ADDICTION THROUGH THE EYES *of a* NURSE

*Rising Above
Adversity
Through Faith*

CHRISTINE N. MALONE MSN, RN

outskirtspress

DENVER, COLORADO

PREFACE

A MOTHER OF two with an innate passion toward other human beings with a dream to take care of the sick and to become a nurse. Refusing to listen to what people told her she could not do but instead believed God. Reaching for her dream by overcoming self-doubt, fighting through the storms, enduring pain, heartaches, rejection, abandonment with faith in God's promises realized in order for her dreams to come to past she must step out and put her faith to work. Her story is meant to instill hope and inspiration in women all over the world to follow their dream and don't quit.

Acknowledgments

I AM THANKFUL to my Heavenly Father who carried me in the mist of my storms and made me realize my fullest potential of what was inside of me. **No good thing does He withhold from those who walk in His statues Psalm 84:11.**

MY BELATED MOTHER Earnestine Newberry who instilled in me courage, strength, and responsibility. **Love the Lord with all your heart, soul, and strength Deuteronomy 6:5**

MY FATHER RAYMOND Newberry who taught me to face fear with boldness whatever I encountered in a given day. **I sought the Lord and He delivered me from all fears Psalms 34:4**

MY TWO SONS Ashshahid Muhammad better known as Bernard and Monterio who encouraged and supported me to write my story, to inspire others to believe in their dream. **Therefore encourage one another with these words 1 Thessalonians 4:18.**

MRS. NELMS LPN instructor, a mentor and friend who planted in me a seed of a warrior. Forewarning as I entered the battlefield against the enemy to never give up no matter what. **I planted the seed, Apollos watered it, but God made it grow 1Corinthians 3:6.**

TERRI MARR RN nurse manager, a God sent angel who supported and encouraged me during those difficult days in RN school. **Do not be discouraged for the Lord is with you Joshua 1:9.**

ME, FOR BREAKING my silence, healing my spirit, moving beyond all fears, struggles, obstacles on to a life full of faith, perseverance, and triumph. I dedicate my life to sharing, teaching and learning, striving for improvement in all that I do. **But with whom revere my name, the sun will rise with healing in its wings and you will go out and leap Malachi 4:2.**

<u>Contents</u>

Introduction

THE FIRST NURSE of color was Mary Eliza Mahoney (May 7, 1845- January 4, 1926). She studied and worked as a professionally trained nurse in the United States, graduating in 1879. She was one of the first black members of an organization which later developed into the American Nurses Association. Mary Mahoney was not just an inspiration to African American women, but to the entire nursing profession. Her drive and passion for nursing helped shape the standards at which the profession has come to expect and continues to develop. I among thousands of other nurses all over the world are what we are today because of the contributions of women like Miss Mahoney. Their strong leadership has allowed women of color to have the courage to step up and follow their same paths.

Encountering many obstacles, challenges, trials in every direction in my pursuit of my dream to become a registered nurse, giving up was not an option. A single mother with a strong desire for a prosperous and successful life rooted inside of me was determined to make something out of my life. After watching my mother day after day struggle labeling herself as a maid working six days a week for very little money I knew

I wanted more. Reflecting back as a little girl writing to God in my diary is when my acknowledgement and a relationship with Him first began. I understood He loved me and wanted what was best for me. But life has a way of just happening to us and we forget all about God and why He placed us on this earth. As a young adult my bible laid in the corner accumulating dust while living a life full of sin and rebellion only calling on God when things were out of control.

~Divine Inspiration: Nothing is more important than knowing the purpose God has for my life and nothing can take the place of knowing Him in the mist of my purpose.~

A young girl being the oldest child I was always taking care of my younger siblings while my parents were away from home. In high school taking a course in Pre-Health introduced me to the nursing and medical field. This sparked a desire to pursue a career in nursing believing God placed in me a compassionate and caring spirit to care for the sick.

~Divine Inspiration: God is the essence of life, always present, always knowing, forever giving us exactly what we need, exactly when we need it.~

All the years of my nursing career there has always been a shortage for nurses in the healthcare industry, but I am thankful it never affected me. I truly love being a nurse. Of course I had my share of trials but it doesn't outweigh the satisfaction I gained from being a nurse. I chose nursing as a career for security not understanding at the time it was my calling to serve humanity. God was working his plan in my life. Nursing with an infinite amount of knowledge allowed me the opportunity to learn something new each and everyday of my career. There were no role models in my family but watching Susan on General Hospital the number one soap opera in America made nursing appear fascinating and glamorous, but finding out later this was far from the truth. Nursing is a world working in the trenches; working tirelessly for the good of our friends, neighbors, and loved ones who are entrusted to our tender, loving and skillful care.

I dreamed of becoming a nurse but having lived a life of abuse, rejection, low self esteem and abandonment couldn't believe this was possible. I carried thoughts of unworthiness and hopelessness, paralyzed by fear, afraid to reach my destiny fulfilling my true mission in life. Addicted to thinking not good enough, not believing God had placed inside me everything I needed to live an abundant life and He would guide me, protect me, and shower me with His goodness.

~Divine Inspiration: I pray that out of His glorious riches He may strengthen me with power through His Spirit in my inner being Ephesians 3:16~

Looking in the mirror unable to see a young woman of substance, beauty, and intelligence, but instead saw lies, criticism and not good enough. Allowing what people said hypnotize me with daily doses of negativity was influencing my beliefs and self-perception of who I am. Not knowing the truth, the misconceptions of the truth manifested itself in my life leaving me feeling unfulfilled and not good enough paralyzing me from moving forward.

Rosa Parks, Harriet Tubman, and Ida B. Wells were women who had to be afraid but did not stop from living a life of truth, freedom and fulfillment. In my mind a registered nurse wasn't for girls like me who came from a poor family whose mother was a maid and father who worked two jobs to make ends meet. My mind believed nursing was for girls who were light-skinned, pretty long hair living in beautiful homes, who wore the finest clothes, belonging to all the sororities offered on campus. The girls who appeared to have high self esteem rolling off their shoulders and parents who held top prestigious jobs.

In a place I never liked being living with a not good enough syndrome, low self esteem kept me in bondage. My mother with only a third grade education did her best to provide us everything we wanted growing up as children but when it came to an education and college degree she knew nothing about. My father dropped out of school at an early age enlisted in the military World War II which held high credibility and prestige in society.

~Divine Inspiration: Be strong and courageous! Do not be afraid and do not panic before them. For the Lord my God will personally go ahead of me. He will neither fail me nor abandon of me Deuteronomy 31:6~

Without any emphasis on a college education or living for God I lived a life full of sin unaware of our Lord Jesus Christ dying on the cross for our sins so we may have eternal life to live a life without sin. I did not realize how much God loved me and bestowed inside me the gifts only he could provide. He wanted to express through me to lead an abundant and blessed life to glorify Him and enjoy Him forever.

~Divine Inspiration: " I am come that you might have life, and that you might have it abundantly John 10:10.

CHAPTER **1**

My Humble Beginning

LIFE WITH IT many storms has a way of putting us down on our knees. Kneeling down on my bended knees, in a dark room, I slowly leaned over onto the sofa and began to cry out to Almighty God, "God help me! Please give me strength." I had lost count the number of times I prayed that prayer. I wanted desperately to quit this self-destructive lifestyle but couldn't. Until you have been addicted to someone or something you can't begin to understand the brokenness, weariness and beaten down life of living in the valley.

~Divine Inspiration: God is our refuge and strength, an ever present help in trouble. He will renew your strength of an eagle and give you wings to fly again Psalm 46:1~

Born the oldest of three children to my parents Raymond and Ernestine Newberry, in Memphis, Tennessee, remembered that cold winter night in January when there was a loud knock on the front door. Opening my eyes immediately to a pit black room, except for the flame from Aunt Lucy's cigarette as she took one last puff hurriedly went to open the door. There stood my mother's frail weak body and my father holding my baby brother wrapped in blankets snuggled real tight. We were so happy to see our new baby of the family coming home. My mother shared with me she had a son born stillborn before I was born. I thought it would have been nice to have an older brother and not carry the burden of being the oldest child.

~Divine Inspiration: Children are a gift from the Lord; they are a reward from Him to bring joy into the world. Psalm 127:3~

We lived in a little white wood two-bedroom house on a hill with a tall flight of steps leading up to our porch. At the tender age of four remembered looking up at our house that seem to reach the sky. We were a complete family; mother, father and three children were my first memories of what a family was suppose to be like. My daddy an ex-veteran of Korean World War II soldier stood 5'5" a small body frame weighing approximate 155 pounds, brown complexion, good-looking, and a very sharp dresser. My mother was a tall, dark complexion, medium built woman with a nice figure and jet black beautiful long hair. She was a stay at home mom while my father worked two jobs. We had the ideal family until my fathers' adulterous affair was revealed one day. My mother and the other woman were expecting a child at the same time. My brother born January 7, 1961 and my half sister was born March 11, 1961. After finding out the truth my mother packed our things and left my father. My fathers' infidelity destroyed our perfect family.

~Divine Inspiration: God heals the broken-hearted and bandages our wounds Psalms 147:3~

Remembering that night as if it were yesterday watched my mother pack all our things and my father driving us to my grandfathers' house. Parking his car on side of the house and getting out he lifted the trunk and proceeded to unload our things onto the porch. There was total silence. I stood on the side of the car not understanding what was happening or why we were being separated from my father. No one was telling me anything and our perfect family ended that night. I never really learned whose choice it was to separate but I often wondered did my mother ever forgive my father for committing adultery. That night I watched my father drive off in his 1961 Buick until I no longer saw the taillights of his car. My heart was heavy and broken to pieces that I was separated from my father. My mother holding my baby brother turned to go into the house and I followed holding my sister's hand. I couldn't help but wonder if I would ever see my father again.

I was crushed and sadden in my soul beyond understanding being separated from my father leaving a deep scar that began to write a story on my suffering heart. A young girl at the tender age of four, I was traveling through my first Valley, a wilderness experience that would follow me all my days. Too young to understand everything but knew my daddy was no longer going to be in the household. I was entering into an environment that was unfamiliar and different from where I came from, a place where my truths, beliefs, foundation all began to take root.

~Divine Inspiration: " Grief cannot shake you if you walk beside me, My hand in yours along the darkness."

No matter how dark the road to life gets God can be a light beneath your feet.~

My grandfather lived in a small one bedroom wood frame house that back in the day we called a shotgun house. One day I asked my mother, "What is a shotgun house?" She said "A house where the rooms go straight back. If you stand in the front door you can see straight through out the back door." My grandmother I never had an opportunity to meet, died the same year I was born at the early age of 42. Everybody use to tell me I looked so much like her. Only seeing old photos she was a tall thin woman with a meek and quiet appearance. I often wondered what she was like.

~Divine Inspiration: Even if my father and mother abandon me the Lord will hold me close Psalm 27:10. My Heavenly Father is always present.~

My grandfather Isaac Blackmon was a tall slender dark skinned man who wore a frown on his face every where you saw him. If you ever met him you would think he was the meanest man in the world. When he spoke everybody listened and obeyed. I was afraid of my grandfather and tried to stay my distance from him as much as possible. He remarried his second wife, Mary Burney a very light-skinned woman half his age with wavy black hair. I use to think she was a white woman until I was older to know the difference. When she moved in the house she brought along her three sons Slick, Rabbit and Shelby.

Born and raised in the country, Hernando, Mississippi my grandfather was the hardest working man I have ever known. He worked from sun up to sundown all of his life on his farm raising chickens, hogs, cows and picking cotton to save enough money to move his family to South Memphis. He moved in a small wooden frame one bedroom house on Kyle Street, where my mother lived until she and my daddy were married. From there he moved to this small one bedroom wood frame duplex house at 1617 South Parkway. This is where my childhood roots begin to develop and mold. My beliefs and values instilled concerning life relationships, communication skills, survival techniques, fears, courage, insecurities, all which play a part of who I am today. Even my self-concept and self-esteem good and bad began to manifest here. I became very withdrawn hardly ever talking to anybody in my grandfathers' house avoiding people as much as possible. I was no longer my daddy's little princess instead I was teased and called "PO LEGS" a name given to me by my grandfather because of my little skinny legs. He thought this was a cute thing to say but it affected my self-esteem making me feel self-conscious and ashamed and I tried to hide my legs wherever I went. Being teased all the time about my skinny legs developed a complex and my self-concept wasn't very high. Every time my grandfather got a chance he pointed at my little legs laughing and screaming out loud,"PO LEGS" causing me to run flopping down on the floor landing on my butt sliding under the table to pout. Under the table was my hiding place. I thought no one could see me there. All the grown folks that came in and out the house called me by that name. A part of me longed to be with my daddy. A piece of my soul died when I was separated from him and I crawled into a shell.

~Divine Inspiration: I am fearfully and wonderfully made; woven together in my mother's womb and wonderfully made Psalm 139:14~

My grandfather raised chickens and plowed a garden around our house like we lived on a farm. All the children living under his roof worked in the garden, tended the chickens, carried gallon jugs of water to plant in the ground next to the crops to keep them watered. Our family pet was a white mule named "Ole John." My uncle Theotria use to ride "Ole John" to school everyday with a wagon attached giving kids in the neighborhood a ride. One day we watched my grandfather take an ax and chop off a chickens' head right in front of us. I was terrified watching the chicken writhing body going round and round in circles for several minutes before it just collapsed on the ground. Then my grandfather picked up the dead chicken taking it inside the house, cleaned it and we ate it for dinner that night. My grandfather worked hard during the week in a mill and boot legged cone whiskey during the evenings, nights, and weekend. He and my step-grandmother were heavy drinkers and there was always a lot of drinking and fighting on the weekends. I hated living here and hoped every day my mother would please find us a better place to live. I missed my daddy so much.

Living in a one bedroom house with my grandfather and sixteen other people under the same roof was atrocious but he never gave my mother the impression we weren't welcome. There was grandfather and his wife Mary, her three sons Alexander who we called Rabbit, William who we called Slick, and Shelby. My mothers' brothers John Willie Blackman, we called him Bubba, Theotria, we called him Deadeye, Charles the baby brother, we called him Jughead, Birthina, my momma middle sister, we called Sugg, Deolla, the baby sister, we called Aunt Dee and Ola Mae my uncle Theotria woman and her two children, Ricky and Patty. One night while sleeping on the floor, in my usual place made with blankets, a rat crawled on my face and bit me on my nose. I sat up in the floor crying with blood dribbling down my face until someone grabbed me and put me in the bed with my two aunts. Aunt Dee my mothers' youngest sister, and Birthina my mothers' mentally handicapped sister, who suffered from seizures and a stroke that left her crippled on her left side. Sleeping in the same bed with them was a nightmare. I would lay there at the foot of the bed at night with my eyes wide open wishing and longing to go back and live with my daddy again where I had my own bed in my own room. I cried myself to sleep every night remembering how it use to be only the five of us in our little white house that sat on a hill. A part of me longed to be with my daddy wishing we could be a family again.

~Divine Inspiration: God will wipe every tear from my eyes, and there will be no more sorrow or pain. Rev. 21:4~

I sat gazing out the front door anxiously waiting for my daddy to come down that dirt road that led up to our house, so happy he did not forget about me. He called my mother and made arrangements for me to spend the weekend with him. I was so excited I was bubbling on the inside. The longer I sat on the sofa gazing out the front door the more intently I stared anxiously waiting to see my daddy so I can tell him all the things I said I would. My daddy always made me feel like his little princess giving me lots of hugs, kisses and smiles and always looked at me admiringly. Even though my mother and father were separated I still loved my daddy and wanted to spend as much quality time with him as possible. He was living with the woman he had the adulterous affair that eventually led to my parents separation. His life with his new family reminded me of how it used to be when we were a family. I felt awkward around his other family, but my daddy always made me feel special and I soon adjusted. One Christmas Ray and Shirley Ann came to visit and my daddy bought Ray a electric train set but he cried the whole time and after opening our gifts he took us home sooner than expected. He was only three and was not use to being away from my mother. I spent weekends with my daddy on a regular basis even walking to school from his house to Hamilton Elementary where I attended school. I loved spending time with my daddy but since the separation our time was limited. The relationship with the opposite-sex parent has the profoundest of bearings on whether or not girls grow up to be happy, serene, healthy, fulfilled individuals. Studies have shown that positive fathering produces well-adjusted, confident and successful daughters who relate well to the men in their lives.

~ Divine Inspiration: "When doubts filled my mind, your comfort gave me renewed hope and cheer." Psalm 94:19~

While living with my grandfather my mother was hardly home working long hours at her older brother Bra'Russells' cafe as a waitress and cook to provide for us a better life saving enough money to rent the house next door to my grandfather. We were so happy and you would of thought we were the Jeffersons "Moving on Up." Instead of having to sleep with two other people I was promoted to the whole sofa in the living room. I no longer had to dodge my two aunts' feet all night while I tried to sleep. I was ecstatic that my mother was able to move us to better living conditions. I was now seven years old and was beginning to notice we didn't have very much and had to do without a lot of things. Aunt Dee moved in with us and babysit us while my mother worked. I can remember when my daddy would pick me up to go to the park Aunt Dee would come alone too. My mother continued working long hours seven days a week and we moved to a house at 963 Ford Place closer to her job. The house was a green wood frame one-bedroom shotgun house too.

~Divine Inspiration: Sail away! Spread my sail toward the -storm and trust in Him who rules the raging seas, put my Hope in God Psalm 42:5~

Moving into our new house my mother didn't mind having her relatives come live with us. When it came to family she was very hospitable and sacrificial and it was always my mother they came to for support and in times of trouble. She started a new job as a maid in a private retirement home for wealthy white women cooking, cleaning, and running errands, which she was highly qualified. She was thankful for a job receiving a real paycheck and no longer getting paid under the table. She work dutifully six days a week wearing her white uniform, white stockings, and white shoes stepping out the door headed to the bus stop with pride and diligence. She seemed to get so much joy from working and didn't have a lazy bone in her body. She was always working around the house, cooking, cleaning, washing and hanging out clothes. Growing up I never saw my mother take a nap during the day hours. I believed she instilled her quality work ethics inside of me and my brother.

~Divine Inspiration: "Work willingly at whatever you

do, as though you were working for the Lord rather than for people." Colossians 1:23~

Living in a different school district I had to transfer from Hamilton School to Cummings Elementary. My teacher Mrs. Turnipseed a very nice black lady would praised my pretty curtsy handwriting, always calling on me to write on the blackboard. She gave me all A's in writing. I had a big crush on the smartest boy in the classroom Melvin Roberts who sat across from me. He won the Spelling Bee Contest receiving a Timex watch for his prize. He was handsome and being smart was a plus. First crushes are innocent, sweet, curious, and hilarious between the opposite sex. I pretended he was my boyfriend but I don't think he really noticed me.

~Divine Inspiration: Love is patient, love is kind. It does not envy, it does not boast, it is not proud 1 Corinthians 13:4~

My father remained in my life and I visited him regularly on the weekends getting to know my sister Debra who was born just a few months after my brother. Everybody said she and I looked more alike than my other siblings. One day my father drove up at our front door and told us all to get in the car, we were going for a ride. You would of thought I had won a million dollars, I was so happy to be going somewhere with my daddy. He drove into the driveway of a big white house with black trimming, a long concrete porch with wrought iron poles and a carport. It was the kind of house I dreamed about living in with my family. We sat in the car amazed, not a word being spoken. My father turned off the ignition in the car and turned toward my mother saying, "This is my house and I want you all to move in with me." My mother just sat there in silence. She was speechless, but her face said it all. She slowly opened her car door and stepped out walking toward the house, still not saying a word. I was so happy inside and felt I had been rescued out of a dungeon by my Prince in shining armor.

Compared to the shotgun wood frame one bedroom houses we had lived all our lives, this house looked like a palace. When we saw our mother enter the house we scrabbled jumping out the car to follow her. Inside it appeared as if my daddy hadn't cleaned since he moved in. There were piles of garbage everywhere. The house had three large bedrooms, living room, separate dining room, and one full bathroom, and a small narrow hall in the center of the house and a large fenced in back yard. This definitely was a step up for us. This was absolutely one of the happiest days of my life and I couldn't wait to move in with my daddy and we would once again be a family. My father convinced my mother to reconcile their marriage and we moved into his new house.

~Divine Inspiration: Are you married? Do you seek a divorce 1 Corinthians 7:27~

My daddy a veteran who fought in Korea War II was good looking and always dressed very sharp wearing a hat everywhere he went being very self conscious about his inherited baldness. He carried himself with a lot pride in his appearance and what people thought mattered. We were never allowed to discuss anything outside the doors of our house and if you forgot and slipped he whip you right there. He worked two jobs and spent all of his leisure time at his favorite place, Sam's Lounge, which was a few blocks away from our house.

If we needed him for anything we knew where to find him. We knew the phone number to Sam's Lounge just like another family member.

Every time I would go to Sam's Lounge my daddy was sitting alone with his bottle of Johnnie Walker red scotch and a glass of ice. I had a lot of respect for my daddy for never bringing his drinking to the house. I never saw him drink alcohol at home around his family and never witnessed him staggering drunk. He never verbally, physically abused my mother, but he was guilty of being a womanizer. My mother found many pictures of him with other women in his truck or shirt pockets and would sat them out on the dresser, never confronting him about it. He was not a stay at home dad and I never remember spending quality time with him except on Christmas and Thanksgiving. I loved my daddy and thought he was the most handsome man in the world and I wanted to marry a man just like him.

~Divine Inspiration: Children's children are a crown to the aged and parents are the pride of their children Proverbs 17:6~

I loved living back in the house with my daddy, bringing back the sweet memories when I was a little girl living on Doris street in our little house that sat on a hill. Aunt Dee only seven older than I was like a big sister came to live with us. We shared and confided in each other with some of our most precious secrets just like girlfriends would do. After two miscarriages and an abusive relationship she never had children of her own, and often told me and my siblings we were her children. When she talked about the lost of her two sons in miscarriages the grief she held onto shown all over her face. I knew if she had a second chance she would do things differently.

~Divine Inspiration: Love is simple when you are around people you are comfortable with. You give love for the sake of love.~

My skin a caramel brown complexion and long black hair that my mother plaited in three big plaits, two in the back and one in the top of my head combed over to the side. All my yearly school pictures first through sixth grade I wore the same style year after year. When turning twelve years old almost a teenager she fixed me bangs to go along with my three big plaits. So accustomed to the same style I was too shy to wear bangs so I pulled them back behind my ear on the way to school. In school my grades were average somewhere between a B- to a C+ student, never making the Honors Roll, but my family thought I was the smartest girl in the whole school with a remarkable memory. Whenever my mother needed to know a phone number of a family member she called on me and I would blurt the number out without hesitation. Then she would brag on me in front of people and a big blush would come over my face. I was a loner most of the time and would stay in the house all day reading, watching television and day-dreaming. After living in our new house a couple of months we met cousins Ruby, Carolyn, and Ray Ray we never knew who lived up the street and we became best friends. They had six other siblings and I admired them for having a large family when it was only three of us. We played all kinds of games; baseball, kickball, four squares, hide and go seek, play acting, skating, and volley ball right in our front yard and in the street. Our house was the house in the neighborhood all the kids from everywhere came to hang out during the summer months while my parents worked.

In the fifth grade I had a big crush on Lewis M. the neighborhood store delivery boy and believed he liked me too by the way he would always look at me. One day while I was riding my bike home from the store through the alley that led to my street he came riding beside me on his bike and stopped, kissed me on the lips and quickly rode off. In total shock I just started to blush. My crush lasted for years but nothing ever happened between us. During my junior high years his sister Barbara and I became best friends even though she was a couple of years older I thought she was such a cool friend. She was a cheerleader and very popular around school. I use to wonder why do she want to be my friend a timid shy girl like me? I can remember the time we went to the Mid South Fair together and we saw a few of her cheerleader friends from school and one of them may a comment, "Is that all you could find to go to the fair with?" Barbara did not respond to the comment but changed the subject trying to prevent me from hearing. We remained friends for a long time until she got a boyfriend and she start spending a lot of time with him.

My cousins moved away and during my sophomore year and I met Pearlie Carter and we became the best of friends. We spent a lot of time at each other's house, walked to school together, spent time after school laughing and talking out on the porch for hours at a time. We remained friends throughout our sophomore year until the school system started busing and we ended up going to different schools. Never having a close relationship with my sister, I spent a lot of time in the house reading every book I could find. I loved to read. I would sat in my parent's room by the window and read for hours at a time. That was my favorite thing to do in the whole wide world.

~Divine Inspiration: Quiet! Be still. "He giveth quietness even in the midst of losing my inner strength and comforts." Mark 4:39~

Shirley was a dark skinned girl with short dusty black hair and medium size frame. My mother always told her how big and pretty her legs were. Hearing my mother praise her big legs when I was labeled with the name "PO LEGS" given to me by my grandfather affected my self-esteem deeply. My mother never told me how cute or pretty I was so I grew up believing my mother loved my sister more impacting my confidence as a young girl tremendously. Shirley was outgoing, typical tomboy, always playing with the neighborhood boys rather than the girls. She had a boyfriend before I did and was never interested in her schoolwork. Living a promiscuous lifestyle she dropped out high school and had three children Tamaki, Zelma and DeRoyce that my mother had to raise. Her life ended tragically at the young age of forty-two in the prison ward at John Gaston with an incurable disease and an inoperable tumor on her brainstem which led to her death. I still remember the day I visited my sister before her death in the women prison talking to her through a glass window on a phone. She had her hair braided in cornrows going to the back and I was admiring her long nails. It was unusual for her to have long nails but every time she was incarcerated she grew long nails. She told me she ate a whole lot of jello while in jail and that's what made her nails grow. I researched jello and found out it's made of horse's hoofs which is made of proteins. I miss my sister Shirley!

~Divine Inspiration: The righteous man does not find encouragement in the opinions of others but in God's word.~

Ray my little brother was a chubby dark skinned boy who was very quiet and kept to himself most of the time. He had a nice grade of hair and wore a big afro. I loved to braid his hair whenever I could talk him into it. He would sat outdoors in front of the house on this concrete block and just watch everybody else do their thing for hours at a time. It was his favorite spot and whenever I looked in that direction I found him sitting there alone quiet in deep thoughts. He never wanted to participate in any of the games with the other kids. Not wanting to leave him out I would always encourage him to join in the fun.

One year he walked all the way home from school in deep turmoil, fearful of opening his report card, afraid of failing the school year. After making it to the corner of our street he gathered enough nerves and opened the report card to find, "Retained to the Fourth Grade" results. Devastated by these results he turned around and walked all the way back to the school and confronted his teacher asking, "Why did you fail me?" I was sad and heartbroken over this devastating dilemma happening in my brother's life, but I knew deep down his report card reflected his performance in school all year. The only consoling I could offer was to be nice to him for a couple of days. The following day he sat on his concrete block for hours not saying anything to anybody. He was never an A student in school and struggled through elementary, high school, college but made a success of his life working as a supervisor for the Memphis Shelby County Correctional Center for over 25 years of hard work and integrity. He also had his own lawn service for many years until he suffered a heart attack that required him to undergo a coronary artery bypass that was successful. Now retired from both jobs he resides in his home with his wife Paula of 26 years, in the process of renovating his home here in Memphis.

~Divine Inspiration: More prayer, more exercising of faith, and more patiently waiting leads to blessings and healing of the body with abundant blessings always.~

CHAPTER 2

Young & Naive

ONE NIGHT WHILE sitting alone on the front porch on a warm summer night a slim light complexion guy approximate 5'9" tall came walking toward me from the apartment complex from across the street. Introducing himself as Larry he asked if he could sit with me. The initial attraction was strong checking him out from head to toe noticing he had the pinkest lips I had ever seen on a black man before. Talking for hours on the porch that night it was obvious we were physically attracted to one another. Recently moved to Memphis, from Mississippi, he was currently staying with two brothers across the street from me. After that night we saw a lot of each another forming a relationship at the age of seventeen my senior year of high school.

Young and naïve I wanted desperately to be in love and to be loved completely by someone. It's what every young girl dream of, finding her Prince Charming doing all the right things and loving her through all her flaws and insecurities. One night while he was home alone we became very intimate, losing my virginity and feeling very vulnerable afterwards but never regretting my choice. I had dreamed of experiencing love and sharing a part of myself with someone else. He came over after school everyday and we made out, got high smoking weed, laughing and playing loud music until my sister and brother came home from school. He would leave to go home and return that night and we would cuddle up on the living room sofa until my momma told him it was time for him to go home.

~Divine Inspiration: When we are vulnerable we fall and our heart open, love comes in: Love is right where you are, whereever you are, in this moment.~

During my senior year 1975 busing became effective in our school district and effected every student from the tenth through twelfth grade. Amongst hundreds of other students I was bused across town to an all white school, Messick High, not understanding the logic behind busing. If parents thought the white students were being provided a better education than the black students why not provide the same opportunities in all the schools instead of separating students from their neighborhood and school district.

One night after a basketball game standing with two of my girlfriends outside waiting for our ride when several guys in a clean shiny gold Cadillac rolled up where we were standing. The driver leaned over the passenger and pointed at me, then parked his car. Coming up to me he introduced himself telling me his name was Fernois. He was a tall light skin guy with a very muscular physique and appeared to be much older. I was fascinated and thrilled he chose me over my girlfriends. He called the next day and came over that night. When I questioned him about his age he pulled out his wallet and showed me his license that confirmed he was twenty years old. For the weekend he asked me to go out with him. I knew the OJays were in town for the weekend so I got dressed up and ready for the concert. He picked me up but instead of taking me to the concert he drove me out to some secluded area and forced me to have sex with him. I tried to fight him off but he was much too strong ripping my new pants and bending my wrist and when I couldn't fight him any longer I surrendered to him. Young and naive to what guys are really interested in I didn't see this coming. Afterwards feeling terribly deceived and robbed of my innocence I wanted to cry but I sat in the seat beside him hurt, betrayed, helpless, angry and disappointed. The drive home there was total silence and seem to be the longest ride I've ever taken in my life. Finally arriving home and getting out of the car without saying a word went in the house straight to my room numb to my surroundings not remembering if anyone saw me come in or not. What I thought was going to be the time of my life turned into a time a piece of my soul was taken away from me. How could I have been so gullible to believe everything he told me?

Date rape occurs when a perpetrator uses physical or psychological intimidation to force a victim to have sex against her will. Most cases of date rape the perpetrator and the victim know each other and is taken less seriously than stranger rape. It could be someone you meet at a party, or someone you love and trust, like your boyfriend. Unfortunately date rape is much more common than you'd believe. Most people think of rape as being committed by a stranger, an attack in a dark alley perhaps but date rape is actually much more common than rape by a stranger. There is controversy that some people believe the problem is overstated and many date rape victims are actually willing and consenting, and others believe that date rape is seriously under reported and almost

most women who are victims of date rape are actually raped. Rape is one of the most underreported crimes and because of this it's difficult to give exact figures. Being one of those unreported cases I will always have a soft heart for the women who cry rape and no one believing her case.

~Divine Inspiration: In some realms of life, shadows of darkness are the places of my greatest strength.~

Lying in bed pretending to be asleep watched my mother trying to adjust my torn zipper in the pants worn that night out with Fernois. Watching her face out the corner of my eye knew she knew exactly what had happened to her daughter. She attempted to fix the zipper but realized it needed more than her motherly touch. Never sharing that awful experience with anybody and hated myself for a very long time for refusing to call it rape. I had began to have feelings for him and I didn't want to believe he could do this to me and deep down thought it was partly my fault. He took advantage of my sweet innocence and raped me. I also hated myself for what I had allowed to happen to me.

~Divine Inspiration: The pain will leave when I learn to see God in everything.~

For two weeks Fernois did not call and when he did I refused to talk to him. He even came to my house and I hid in the back telling my sister to tell him I wasn't home. I really didn't know what to say to him. I had many mixed emotions, I wanted to hate him for what he did to me and I also wanted him to pursue me. Although when I missed my cycle and began experiencing morning sickness I became worried and accepted his call telling him my suspicions. He stopped calling altogether. I tried calling him but the people who answered the phone always said he wasn't there. Two months passed and I still had no period and morning sickness continued. I was hoping and praying I wasn't pregnant but I was experiencing all the signs and symptom and I knew deep down I was. How could I let this happen on a one night stand or call it what it is a one night rape. On top of all the hurt and pain of being raped and abandoned I was now pregnant. This was definitely a valley experience in my life.

~Divine Inspiration: God is in the midst of me, I will not be moved; God will help me when morning dawns Psalms 46:5~

Statistics reveal that ten percent of girls 19 and under do get pregnant. I guess I fall into this statistic. I was seventeen and pregnant with my first child. Young girls desperately need a mothers' support, guidance, love and non-judgmental role model to guide them in the right direction during these vulnerable and precious years. While out one night with friends at the Mid South Fair trying to lift myself out of the valley I had been living since that awful night, I looked up and there was Fernois with a woman and two small kids. I thought this can't be happening. I thought this must be his wife. The kids looked just like him with same skin complexion, and the woman was very pretty with a beautiful figure. Before he saw me, I quickly turned and went in the opposite direction, still hurting, ashamed and bitter. I couldn't bare to face him. I realized at that moment I was just someone he used, took advantaged of and went on with his life like I never existed. When my pregnancy was confirmed by a doctor I wasn't sure who the daddy was. When I told Larry about my pregnancy he never questioned if it was his baby or not. He never knew anything about my relationship with Fernois.

~Divine Inspiration: Take a moment to take a deep breathe. Allow what you are feeling and thinking. The moment you cannot take it anymore, reach down on the inside and let out a scream. Then draw on your power, your strength, the divinity of life and tell yourself, "This is going to make me stronger."~

CHAPTER **3**

The Lying Game

The lying game has been around for years and probably will be around for many more to come. Women and men get involved into relationships for the wrong reasons and it turn out to be pretty ugly. Many times men can be very deceitful and take advantage of a young naïve girl and rob her of her purity then move on to the next innocent victim. This game can go both ways, because there are young ladies who go out and pick a prey and deliberately get pregnant so she can become a mother to have someone to love and to love her back. Of course these people are not sleeping with just one person and this is when the lying game come into play. The woman has the power to say whomever she wants the daddy of her baby to be. Isn't that something! God has a sense of humor. He has given the woman the power to be the ruler over the earth as the creator to multiply and populate the earth. Nobody else has that power but Him. Sin will make you lie and cheat and mess up your whole life and it will literally destroy peoples lives. Every sin has its due consequences and I didn't realize one day I would have to reap what I had sown.

~Divine Inspiration: Some people reman in dysfunctional relationships just to be able to say they stayed. Or they might stay to say, "We did our best. I tried really hard. I gave all I had to give." Or we may stay hoping against all odds that things will get better.~

The birth of my first child was the most painful and empowering experience of my life. Experiencing high blood pressure during labor put me at risk for complications so I had to endure natural childbirth. The whole experience literally took my breath away. My son was born a perfectly healthy baby on February 16, 1976 in John Gaston Maternity Ward weighing 6 pounds and 4 ounces. He had slick jet black hair, light complexion and could of easily pass for a white baby. The next morning the nurse entered my room to complete my baby's birth certificate, something I hadn't given much thought, with so much happening with his birth and all. She asked me what is my baby's name and the father's name. I froze for a moment, sat up in bed and slowly reached for the form and began to fill in the blanks. I named my baby Bernard and I put Larry as his father. As far as I was concerned Larry was the father. Fernois was no longer in my life. A young girl at the age seventeen, not fully developed emotionally or physically, unsure of who I am, I did the only thing I knew to do. There was no one I could go to, too ashamed to talk to anyone about the abuse I had endured. I was young and naïve but old enough to know I was doing the wrong thing. I didn't realize the repercussions of this deceitful act and where it would lead my life.

The mother-daughter relationship between me and my mother was emotionally distant, withholding, inconsistent, hypercritical with very hurtful remarks throughout my teen and young adult years which undermined my self-esteem and self confidence. I honestly hated her for the way she treated me but continued to love her as my mother. Being a shy and timid vulnerable young girl easy to sway down the wrong path I needed to know that my mother loved me. I needed her to boost my self esteem and confidence with seeds of encouragement. As an adult I've learned that every woman commonality is the discovery that each of us, is not alone and have had a mother who can't or won't love us. Knowing these facts lifts some of the hurt but I never understood how a mother would not love her child no matter what.

A young girl needing her mother's love tried convincing myself that my mother loved me she just didn't know how. I constantly received no validation or self-worth, no expression of love, no support or guidance in the choices I made in life. I told myself I had to learn how to believe and love myself.

~Divine Inspiration: When you tell a lie, you become enslaved by a lie. The lie will control your life. The lie determines what you do, how you do it. When you are a slave to a lie, you become the one who keeps the Master alive.~

A baby is such a beautiful and exciting creature to bring into the world and I am so grateful God used me as His vessel to birth my sons into the world. Children are a gift to mothers and God allows it to happen for a reason. A frightened and uncertain young girl making hard decisions that would change my life forever was never questioned by my parents about who was the father of my child. Living at home with my parents on government assistance which provided me with in-home childcare, allowing me the opportunity to enroll in college when Bernard turned six months old, to pursue my nursing career to become a registered nurse.

~Divine Inspiration: Even though you thought you wasn't good enough O Child of little faith, God will see you through.~,

CHAPTER 4

I'sssss Married Now!

WHEN BERNARD TURNED a year old Larry and I began looking for our own place, finding a small one bedroom yellow wood run down apartment house for $75.00 a month. At the time receiving government assistance welfare the government came after Larry for not paying child support through the juvenile court system and he went to jail. After going to jail twice and his family bailing him out they were very upset and start suggesting we get married. Young and naïve the idea of marriage was wonderful even though Larry's behavior showed all the signs he was not husband material. I began planning and orchestrating to make a marriage happen seeking love and validation from a man. Even though the doubts weighed in my mind I kept telling myself he would change after we were married. Why is it that women don't pay attention to their intuition and follow their first mind? Research has proven that our intuition is a powerful force and is more fact that foolery. It is often an unwelcome visitor but should be received and respected. Larry was hesitant and postponed my plans but I was very persistent and in a few months we were married at the Court House in City Hall downtown. I can remember that rainy day so clearly, riding home on the bus elated and blissful that I was married now, a real wife.

~Divine Inspiration: Accept the way God does things. For who can straighten what He has made crooked Ecclesiastes 7:13.~

Moving out of my parents' home was frightening at first now having to make grown up decisions, living on my own, paying bills and managing a house with a family. The rush for freedom was quickly replaced with anxiety and many responsibilities. I continued with my education at Shelby State Community College while Larry worked at a welding company. Larry never had a problem finding a job, but consistently got fired due to his drinking problem which seem to get worse especially on weekends. I noticed the drinking early on in our relationship thinking it was just social drinking not realizing it would interfere with his job or jeopardize our relationship. I was offered a job by Uncle Theotria's wife who was an assistant manager at a hotel to clean rooms. I took the job because I wanted to make my own money and not depend on Larry for everything. I worked there for nine months then moved on to work in a factory working on an assembly line packing Christmas paper. I was only there for two weeks due to a fight breaking out between the supervisor and one of the employees. Even though I was innocent, everybody on the assembly line was fired. Learning a priceless lesson of I was guilty by association. Without a job I applied for welfare government assistance again thanking God for government assistant programs during those difficult times. Welfare programs are state regulated programs for those who live under the minimum accepted level of income determined by each state. After being on welfare a couple of months Larry told me about a factory The United Uniform Company. They made men uniforms and hired only women employees. With many years of sewing experience I applied for the job and was hired on the spot.

~Divine Inspiration: My Grandma said, "Trouble has a way of preparing me for better things in my future. But most of all trouble was building my faith and trust about the power of God~

On this new job I was expected to sew 75 dozens pockets on men uniform shirts daily to reach production to pass my probationary period. I eventually was reaching a 100 dozens a day without any problem. I met four sisters and we all became good friends. I enjoyed talking with other women outside the home learning how they handled their relationship problems. I learned I wasn't the only one going through difficult times. After a year Larry and I were able to purchase our first car, a 1972 green four door Maverick. The car was so clean without any dents or scratches. It felt like we had a brand new car. When Larry was sober he was a totally different man and whatever I wanted he agreed, but while drinking he transformed from Dr Jekyll to Mr. Hyde.

CHAPTER **5**

Abuse Is Ugly

THE PHYSICAL ABUSE actually started before I left my parents' home but I ignored the signs and accepted it because this was normal behavior where I was raised. As a little girl growing up in my grandfathers' house domestic violence and heavy drinking was as natural as waking up in the morning. I saw all the women in my environment; my grandfathers' wife, my Uncle Theotrias' wife, and Aunt Dee all endure physical and verbal abuse. A growing body of literature shows that children who have been exposed to domestic violence are more likely than their peers to experience abuse in some form. Children who are raised in abusive homes learn that violence is an effective way to resolve conflicts and problems. Growing up around so much abuse thinking this is what everybody do to handle their problems or misunderstandings this was how a relationship between a man and a woman was suppose to be. There is no such thing as fairy tale love.

~Divine Inspiration: In relationships it is possible to stay long after it is healthy or wise to do so. To stay for the sake of staying could hurt you beyond the physical,

mental, and emotional pain, there is the damage that is done to your spirit too.~

I was learning life is no fairy tale and there are no Prince Charming who would ride in on a shiny black horse and sweep me off my feet. Larry drinking got worse along with the verbal and physical abuse every weekend that always ended in arguing and fighting. My family came to my rescue time and time but I did not want to hear what they had to say. I always went back to him. When things became terribly bad I was too embarrassed to talk to any one. I would leave Bernard over to my parents house on the weekend because I didn't want him to see the drinking and abuse.

Early one morning around 3:00 am Larry came home after being out all night intoxicated. Hardly able to stand he began an argument over why dishes were left in the sink then asked me to fix him something to eat. I told him NO, which led to a fight. He beat me in my head with his fists hitting me multiple times causing my head and face to swell all over. The next morning waddling in self-pity and low self-esteem went over to my parents' house and when my mother took one look at my face without saying a word she jumped in her car and drove to my house and threatened Larry to keep his hands off me or else. The physical abuse stopped but the verbal abuse and his excessive drinking continued. In my distorted mind I thought this was my fault and if only I could be a better wife he would change. My not good enough addiction inflated my low self esteem causing me to accept the domestic abuse week after week. Being a not good enough addict everything I did wasn't good enough, always beating myself up. There was something inherently wrong for me to accept this abusive treatment, believing in my addictive mind, I was not good enough.

One night Larry came home in one of his usual drunkard state. Trying to distance myself from him I went in the living room minding my own business when he came and sat in my lap with his body facing mind. Weighing barely 95 pounds I couldn't bulge no matter how hard I pushed and squirmed underneath him. He pointed his finger in my face saying some degrading and obnoxious things criticizing me on what a terrible wife I was. Enraged with anger I yelled, "Get off me." I yelled those words over and over. He continued pointing his finger saying the same demeaning and degrading things over and over. Looking at his finger only inches from my face I opened my mouth as wide as I could and bit down on his finger until my teeth collided with the bone in his finger. He let out a loud holler and with all the strength in my body I pushed him to the floor grabbing the wooden broken coffee table leg and began beating him in his face and head striking him with the screws that stuck up multiple times over and over until blood start flying everywhere. Hollering and screaming while holding both hands up he tried to shield his face and head but the blows were coming to fast. I was able to overpower him due to his drunkard state. I tossed the wooden leg down on the floor running out the front door as fast as I could run to the end of the long front yard that led to the sidewalk. Turning quickly to look behind me I saw him busting through the screen door with blood gushing down his face with a dazed look on his face running and staggering toward me. I started running as fast as my legs could carry me. When he came to the end of the yard to turn in my direction he slipped on the wet grass and hit the ground. Every time he tried to get up he slipped again, finally giving up he laid there on the ground.

I ran all the way to my parents house and stayed there all

night. They knew I was having another fight and didn't ask any questions. Embarrassed and ashamed of my relationship deliberately avoided any conservations from anyone. The next day Larry called to tell me his brother Eddie had taken him to the Emergency Room to get his head and hand stitched up. Returning home later that same day found him sitting in the middle of the bed watching television with gauze dressing wrapped around his hand and entire head revealing only his eyes, nose and mouth. He looked at me and said "Girl that doctor said you was trying to kill you." When he was sober he hardly spoke two words. I felt some remorse seeing him bandaged up like that, but when you get sick and tired you sick and tired. He never laid his hands on me or put his finger in my face, but the excessive drinking continued on the weekends.

Larry recuperated rather quickly and we put the whole incident behind us reconciling our relationship. Tired of the little run down wood apartment house we were living in we upgraded to a nicer place. We moved to the SkyLane luxury apartments, equipped with all the finest commodities costing us double the rent that we were already paying. I was so excited hoping our relationship would move to another level. But the heavy drinking and the verbal abuse continued and I endured it. I put him out so many times I lost count. He would call repeatedly apologizing, saying he was sorry, and I surrendered after listening to the sweet talk for hours. Being apart from him for more than two days became unbearable and emotionally distraught. I experienced love withdrawals just as an addict would from drugs with strong mixed feelings of confusion not knowing what to do. I had become a prisoner of my own abuse.

~Divine Inspiration: If God gave you the vision he will give you the provision. Allow courage to replace fear and let your dream pull you forward.~

Once while we were apart I went out partying on the weekend with my sister and friends when I received a phone call from Larry that my house was on fire. Immediately leaving my parents' house rushing to my apartment found my front door knocked in, my bedroom furniture badly damaged, and my refrigerator raided of all the meat out my freezer. I was never informed by the fire department what caused the fire assuming it started in the apartment underneath me causing the flames to reach the roof of my apartment. The people who lived there were not home at the time of the fire. My family believed Larry was the perpetrator but I really didn't have any proof he was guilty of anything and being a love addict I couldn't see the signs even if someone hit me over the head. Deep down I didn't want to believe he would do such a horrendous thing.

~Divine Inspiration: The peace of God, which transcends all understanding. God declares this peace to be the inheritance of those who have learned to rest only in Him Philippians 4:7~

Moving back with my parents until a new apartment was ready I saw how the love between them was dead. My mother slept in the den with my little brother and treated my daddy with so much hostility, bitterness and resentment. They soon separated with my mother moving to a four room wood frame duplex house painted a pale yellow and my father moved to a brick duplex apartment. After settling in my new apartment I had it in my heart to go forward with my life starting over with just my son. I was tired of all the abuse, name-calling, and disrespect. My income was not enough to keep the luxury apartment found a small one bedroom brick duplex for $75.00 a month on Wabash Street two streets over from where my father lived. Still sick with my love addiction Larry repeatedly called and he was back in my life again. You would think I had learned a lesson, but that's what an addiction to love will do. Things always starting out good between us but he gradually went back to the same old behavior. I realized he really hadn't changed and the heavy drinking and abuse was still there continuing on that vicious cycle.

~Divine Inspiration: Love between a man and woman is a feeling and a commitment. It is feeling of desire and devotion that draws two people together. It is a commitment to remain together no matter what happens to the feelings.~

CHAPTER 6

The Awakening

WORKING OUTSIDE THE home I looked forward to being around other women I could hear their perspective on relationships and other things women dealt with. The four sisters I befriended one was married, one was living with a man for 15 years, one lived alone, and one lived with her parents. We all worked on the same assembly line and would gather in the bathroom on cigarette breaks sharing some of our most intimate and confidential stories about our lives. Listening to other women stories I discovered, I wasn't alone, other women were victims of domestic abuse too. But their stories wasn't as horrific as mine. I was selective in the the things I shared, too ashamed to share about the physical and verbal abuse I endured almost daily. Some women value a relationship with a man more than their own dignity and respect for themselves and tend to hold on to what is familiar and comfortable even though it isn't healthy for them. Even though the relationship is not healthy or wise women stay hoping against hope that things will get better, just so they will not be alone. I begin to wonder why remain in a relationship that is emotionally draining with a man who do not love and respect me for the Queen I am. Why stay in a relationship where I was to ashamed what was happening to me? Something inside of me began to want more than a man who just lived for the week-end, or the next bottle of alcohol, or some dope to smoke. I desired a man with a vision, a dream, goals the same as mine.

~Divine Inspiration: Begin to learn, explore new horizons, begin to grow, begin healing and transform.~

Living in a dysfunctional toxic relationship continuing to sacrifice my heart and soul enduring years of abuse found myself getting pregnant for the second time. During the pregnancy my feelings and respect for Larry had diminished no longer wanting him near me. Things just wasn't the same. Research has proven women experience emotional changes due to the hormonal changes in their bodies. I guess my hormones were unbalanced or I was growing tired of a relationship that seem to destroy me emotionally and spiritually heading nowhere. I had to eventually quit my job and unable to depend on Larry I applied for welfare and food stamps for financial support. Experiencing life outside the home working amongst other women sharing our life stories I began to realize I wanted more out of life. I was sick and tired of the drinking, the argu-ing, the meaningless fighting every weekend. I want to be my own woman. I didn't want somebody trying to control my life. I realized Larry and I didn't have anything in common as far as life's goals and dreams. We weren't on the same plane. I was no longer attracted to him nor needed him as much as I thought. It was disheartening to realize how much of myself, time, and energy was invested into someone who didn't have a vision, but lived only for the weekend.

Sitting at home all alone feeling sorry for myself wasn't

sure if I wanted to go through with my pregnancy began flipping through the yellow pages searching for an abortion clinic. Dialing the number to an abortion clinic and in two rings a woman picked up the phone. After telling her my situation, listened as she went through all the details of an abortion step by step. I begin to think, "An abortion is a sin, murder, and displeasing to God". I told her I would call her back. But I never did. I decided to put it in God's hand and he would work things out. In God eyes an unborn child is a living human baby.

~Divine Inspiration: "Children expresses innocence, curiosity, and love that is so precious. They enter the world depending and relying on their parents to be there to guide and comfort them in all their needs."~

Pregnant with my second son I tried to eat healthy, taking all my prenatal vitamins, drinking plenty of water, getting plenty of rest, and making all of my monthly clinic appointments gave birth to healthy baby boy Monterio on August 1, 1981 at 9:30 pm. Praise God! He was very light complexion, head full of jet black hair, weighing 6 pounds and 6 ounces. My daddy thought for sure he was going to be born on his birthday which is August 2. After Monterio's birth Larry spent some time with his son, but his excessive drinking and abusive behavior did not stop. One night while fighting he hit me in my left eye so hard I thought I would never see out that eye again. Holding my eye with both hands went down on the bed curled in a fetal position screaming and crying. Bernard watching in the corner of the room let out a scream so loud that went all through my soul. He continued to scream until Larry turned and walked away.

That moment I knew I could no longer accept this kind of abuse or behavior promising myself to never let him back in my life. I was breaking this love addiction before I or my children were seriously harmed. If I didn't do it for myself I had to do it for my children. I loved my children more than I loved having a man in my life.

Larry called repeatedly but this time I didn't answer like I had done in the past. He didn't realize it was completely over, but I did. I knew in my head not my heart it wasn't going to get any better. He wasn't the man I needed and wanted. Entangled in a love sick addiction, I made up my mind that day at that moment I was finish taking the abuse. I allowed myself to endure the abuse for seven years and now it was time for me to accept the cold hard truth, he was never going to change. He is not the man for me. I had poured out my heart and soul for so long hoping and waiting on love that never came. I expended a great deal of myself, my time and energy chasing someone that did not love or respect me as the Jewel God created. Crawling from under this sick love addiction I begin to understand Larry was suffering from a deep self hate and low self-esteem eating him up on the inside, concealing it with the alcohol and drugs. He wasn't capable of loving when he couldn't love himself. I suffered from severe low self-esteem and not good enough addiction and accepted the abuse because I really did not love myself enough. My self esteem and love for myself was minus zero and no one told me otherwise. As a young girl searching for love tried to find it in a relationship with a man.

~Divine Inspiration: When you have reached a point of no return in a situation, it means you have given all you can give, taken all you can take, you know there is

no hope of things to get better, this is not a bad thing. It is simply time to move on.~

Now that I had moved on emotionally torn in my soul feeling hopeless as if all my dreams had gone down the drain, I asked myself, "Why did you remain in a toxic relationship for that long enduring such demeaning treatment and disrespect?" Reminiscing back over the times when Larry was sober he was loving and kind. These were the times I looked forward to. I will now call them, "little nuggets of love" of a love addict. This is why so many women remain in abusive and domestic violent relationships, for another sprinkle of "little nuggets of love" usually after abuse, which becomes addicting. After enduring poor treatment from a man over a long period of time we become so deeply addicted to these "little nuggets of love" desperately wanting to be loved. Living with low self esteem, not loving myself, didn't think I deserved to be loved. When Larry would dish out a "little nugget of love" I crave for the next nugget no matter how much abuse I had to endure to get it. It is absolutely sick that's what it is, SICK. Addicted to love. It was unbelievably hard to walk away from and start a new life but by the grace of God I gained enough strength and courage to look forward and no matter how hard, not to look back.

~Divine Inspiration: The sorrows of life causes us to rise toward God!~

My emotional scars and mixed emotions were in need of a whole lot of healing. I mourned and cried my eyes out for months after the separation. To finish answering my question why I stayed so long in a relationship that was toxic enduring years of abuse? I thought he would change. I thought I could make him love me. I was afraid I couldn't take care of my boys alone. I didn't want to be alone. I wanted to show him I could be the wife he wanted.

~Divine Inspiration: No man is worth your tears. Every woman deserves to be treated and respected like a Jewel in which God made her.~

In deep sorrow waddling in self pity for months while every fiber of my soul ached I turned to God for strength. I prayed that God would break me free from my stronghold. Emotionally tied to a dysfunctional toxic relationship that held me in its grips for seven long years was blinded by a false love and paralyzed by fear of being alone. Throughout the relationship I would ask myself, "Are you receiving what you deserve in this relationship? Is this a nurturing relationship for you? Are you dying slowly in this relationship?" Deep down I always knew the answers to these questions were no. The truth was I felt unloved and unappreciated. But thank God I came to my senses realizing I deserved better. In Gods eyes I am a Queen marvelously created for his purpose. He is a good and faithful God who love me and does not want me to accept less than the best. Even while living a sinful and disobedient life God's grace and mercy was with me all alone. I put the enemy of fear behind me and put forth my faith in God a Higher Power greater than myself to bring me out of my pit because I could not do it for myself.

Always believing in God I kept a personal journal that I wrote letters to him all the time. I was first introduced to God through my mothers' oldest sister Aunt Vinnie. Aunt Vinnie was different from all the other grown ups in the family. She was married to a preacher who had his own church, denomination Church of God and Christ. When school was out she would call me to the phone interrupting my playtime outside with the other kids or my reading time in my parents room and read the bible to me over the phone. One night she invited my family to a revival at her church. When we arrived I didn't know what to expect. She and all the mothers of the church put me in the center of a circle and start turning me round and round while they shouted religious rhetoric over and over until something came over me knocking me to the floor. My mother later told me that was the Holy Spirit. While Growing stronger in my struggles of adapting to living alone I learned to trust in God more and more. I thank God I did not become one of the statistics 46% of female homicide victims who are killed by current or former spouses. The numbers were even higher for partners who leave their spouses. When I see other women in an abusive relationship I say "Lord there go I."

~Divine Inspiration: "Be strong and of good courage; do not be afraid, nor be dismayed, for the Lord your God is with you where ever you go"Joshua 1:7~

My Uncle Bubba was found dead lying across his bed wearing only his underpants and a pair of socks a few months after my son Monterio was born. He died of a heart condition following a recent coronary bypass. Being my favorite uncle it was so sad to find him dead like that. Well-known all over Memphis nobody messed with him not even the police. He was my mothers' oldest brother and there wasn't a day passed he didn't come over to our house looking for something to eat. Every time you saw him he had a roll of money in his pockets but he just love to eat at our house. My momma was known for her delicious cooking and she could cook anything. Uncle Bubba always kept everybody laughing, but I got the most joy when I saw a smile come across his face or a laughter jump out his mouth. He was such a serious man always focused on his next hustle. He was a real live hustler never having a job all of his 50 years. He didn't have any close friends but was known by everybody. There were three things you would never see him without; a roof over his head, a woman, and money in his pocket.

He paid cash for his house putting it in my brother's name and after his death my mother moved into the house. It wasn't in the best conditions but at least it was paid for and she didn't have to worry about a mortgage. My brother was away in school and my mother lived there alone until she met a man named James Gamble who went by the name Hop, a big time gambler known all over Memphis. He worked for a realty rental company repairing and preparing rental property but on the weekend he ran my mothers' house like a café in the front and a gambling house in the back. Loud music vibrated throughout the house with people drinking, gambling, smoking, frying fish, and dancing until two and three o'clock in the morning. Everybody came to my mothers' house on the weekend.

My mothers' house was my home away home and every weekend I got dressed up and partied until wee hours of the morning trying to drown out the emotional pain after breaking up with Larry. Everyday I struggled to transition my life from sharing it with someone for years to hoping he would call again. The addiction to love stronghold still had it pangs in me and no one could possibly understand my pain. I tried so hard to suppress the pain with my drinking during this emotional affliction. Now I know God was showering me with His trials to serve His purpose, and that weeping may remain in the night rejoicing comes down the road. He saw the precious rock of faith in the core of my nature and these trials is to refine me into purity and beauty. One night after leaving my mothers' house driving home from a long night of partying I literally hit a woman crossing the street in my 1974 old model green Maverick. Bernard standing behind me on the back seat screamed, "Momma you hit that woman." The woman fell to the pavement but immediately jumped up and staggered on her way never acknowledging me at all as if nothing happened. At 2am in the morning I figured she must be in a worser state than me.

~Divine Inspiration: If you intentionally seek out sinners as your companions, they will lead you down paths that take you from God~

Living in a dysfunctional toxic relationship damaged my self esteem and self worth to the point I felt unattractive, uninterested, and unworthy of ever finding love. I still yearned for my ex-husband, holding on to the emotional scars not knowing how to begin to heal. My first step was to understand that it wasn't my fault. Women in abusive relationships tend to blame themselves for the abuse when in actuality there is never any justification for abuse and every woman deserve to be treated with dignity and respect. Surviving domestic abuse and healing from domestic violence is a process and it doesn't happen over night. Trying so hard to pick myself up and go forward, to love and respect myself and leave all the memories of a bad marriage behind waddled in deep depression struggling to get through each day. Trying to build a new relationship after an abusive marriage was tough, connecting with men ignoring all the red flags searching for the kind of love I dreamed about as a young girl. The kind of love that would sweep me off my feet. The Cinderella type love. I found out this kind of love doesn't exist and I was living in a fantasy world. My dream of getting married to my Prince Charming and having kids living in a house with a white picket fence was crushed after living in an abusive marriage. I started to realize I didn't need a man to validate who I am. I thank God for bringing me this far. I couldn't have made it without his love and guidance, nor without my mustard seed of faith that was beginning to grow inside of me.

~Divine Inspiration: The grace of God does come forth to bring rest and restoration to our soul until we completely reach the point of stillness in Him.~

CHAPTER 7

Choosing a Better Life

TIRED OF WADDLING in self pity, living a life of alcoholism and partying every single weekend, heading for self-destruction I was sick of my life and I wanted to fulfill my dream. Unaware at the time that in order to go forward with my life, to go after my dream I must release all the resentment and unforgiveness harboring in my heart in order for God to forgive me also. Living in an one bedroom duplex apartment it was time for a larger place for me and my two boys. I was tired of relying on government assistance for welfare and food stamps dealing with all the rude social workers who looked with condemnation, judgmental and talking down to me. I was in a place I no longer wanted to be but afraid to move forward envisioning obstacles, struggles, and challenges up ahead. During a three month recertification period disagreeing with the case worker final analysis of my allotted benefits, I asked," Are you sure this is all I suppose to receive?" She responded nonchalantly, "Yes ma'am." Angrily I blurted out, "This is not enough for me to live off." She looked up saying, "This check is not meant for you to live off. It's only meant for you to survive." I was speechless. That statement stung me to the very core of my soul. I drove all the way home meditating on those awful words that flowed so easily from the social worker's mouth. Those words sparked a flame inside my soul that created a new energy to fight. To fight for my dream, my vision God placed in me. That lady was absolutely right. Why should the government make my life comfortable while I sat at home everyday doing nothing?

~Divine Inspiration: When you love yourself, you honor yourself and others who bring the truth. The truth gives me exactly what I need in order to express who I truly am.~

Later that day I contacted Sea Isle Vo-Technical School to inquire about their LPN twelve month program. A pre-entry California Achievement exam was required with a passing score of 81% to qualify and be accepted into the program. My score was too low to qualify and the administrator of the program counseled me encouraging me to take the nursing assistant course. Thinking I had to start somewhere I enrolled in the nursing assistant three month program completing the course successfully in 1982 receiving a certificate at graduation. This was my first accomplishment and I couldn't wait to start living my life. I thank God for that social worker. She inspired my soul to want to do more. Even though my circumstances appeared overwhelming and difficult, I mustered up a little faith and decided I must go forward. Something had to change and the only way it was going to change is if I made it happen.

~Divine Inspiration: None of my trials go unnoticed

by God. God is peace, joy, strength, power, abundance that you desire in your life.~

Successfully completing the nursing assistant program I applied for a job in the hospitals, nursing home, doctors offices but there were no jobs available. I went to Walgreen Drugstore, where my cousin Ruby worked and she helped me get a job as a cashier. Being shy as I was working on the front register was a challenge interacting with the public. Thrilled beyond words to have a job even though there were all kind of strife with other women I tried to have a positive attitude. However there were no problems with my boss, I actually think he liked me. I found out working with people and money you have to be extremely careful, because people will outright lie to your face. One night while working on the front register feeling good and confident, a tall slender black guy came through my line with a quart of beer and handed me a $5 bill. When I returned his $3 and change he stated, "You didn't give me enough change back, I gave you a $20 bill." I immediately replied, "You gave me a $5 bill." He became very loud and obnoxious, causing me to become extremely uncomfortable shaking and trembling all over. I even questioned myself, "What did he give me?" My manager rushed over to my register to handle the situation. We were always told to put all large bills larger than a $10 bill, checks, and coupons under the money drawer. The manager looked under my drawer and there were no $20 bills. That solved everything. I was so embarrassed! Why didn't I think to do that? Then there was another time a short thin black guy came through the line with a quart of beer and holding a brown paper sack full of pennies spreading them all out onto the counter. While counting all those pennies, I watched out the corner of my eye as the line grew longer and longer with all the angry and disgusted faces gazing directly at me. In this case my manager rushed to open another line seeing how nervous and sweaty I was. Nonetheless working there only six months I was let go as a result of my money drawer being consistently short. Although I wasn't stealing money but at the end of my shift my receipts, coupons and checks did not balance out. God had something better in mind for me.

~Divine Inspiration: The peace of God, which transcends all understanding. God declares this peace to be the inheritance of those who have learned to rest only in Him Philippians 4:7~

Henceforth my next job a teachers' aide at the Board of Education I worked enthusiastically alongside teachers in the classroom environment. One important virtue necessary to being a school teacher is PATIENCE. As a result of the opportunity to work in the school system I understand and appreciate what teachers actually go through inside of a classroom setting was a phenomenal experience. Fifty percent of the classroom time is spent trying to control and discipline disruptive, rowdy, misbehaved students. All in all, this experience changed my heart toward all educators in the school system and truly believe they are underpaid and unappreciated for what they do in the educational system. Staying in that position for nearly two years it was important for me to realize this was not what God had for me. I reapplied for the Licensed Practical Program at Sea Isle Vocational School and successfully passed the California Achievement Test with a score greater than 81 and was accepted in the nursing program starting January 6, 1986.

> ~*Divine Inspiration: Never give up on your dream!*
> *Oh God, things will not be hard since you tread my path*
> *before me. And for my good this thing must be His grace*
> *sufficient.*~

CHAPTER 8

My Dream

THE PROFESSION OF nursing began in the early roots of Florence Nightingale whom set the bar in regards to giving excellence in nursing practice delivered with a commitment to passion and love. Nursing embodies core values such as honesty, responsibility, human dignity, compassion, and love for the sick. Nursing requires prolong training, competence, and skilled professional behavior. Notably believing nursing is my God given purpose and ministry to serve and care for the sick in their time of need. There have always been reports of a nursing shortage and a high demand for nurses in all specialties; hospitals, nursing homes, and education. After 25 years a shortage remain across the country while nursing schools and universities expand enrollment levels to meet the rising demand for nursing care.

However as a young girl recall nurses and teachers occupations held by women were held in high regards by the American people. Whereas research reveals in the 1940s and 1950s these occupations were held 99% by Caucasian women in hospitals and classrooms. Today teachers in the school system are indeed special and very well needed all over the world. Nursing is an occupation chosen by women more than men and much needed also. Women femininity is an integral part of caring for others, value family and relationships, more than men. There are 2,824,641 registered nurses and 690,038 licensed practical nurses in the US. About 23.6% of LPNs are black or African American (non-Hispanic); 3.6% are Asian; 7.5% are Hispanic or Latino; 0.6% are American Indian or Alaskan Native; and 1.4% categorize themselves as two or more races. Approximately 9.9% of RNs are black or African American (non-Hispanic); 8.3% are Asian; 4.8% are Hispanic or Latino; 0.4% are American Indian or Alaskan Native; and 1.3% categorize themselves as two or more races. (*MinorityNurse.com., Data/Statistic, The Office of minority Health, 2012*).

I was starry-eyed and excited about starting the nursing program, a career I had dreamed about all my life. A career that would train and prepare me as a professional to protect, promote health and prevent illness and injury to alleviate suffering of the sick. The AFDC (American Families of Dependent Children) welfare program offered the Victory program for women receiving welfare who desired to enroll in school providing all the expenses and cost of the nursing program including; books, uniforms, lunch money, transportations funds, and daycare services. This is one of those blessings where God made my rough edges smooth. One stipulation required was satisfactory passing grades and attending class Monday through Friday 8:00am- 4:30 pm without more than two absences. I had recently purchased a 1972 Ford Pinto for reliable transportation thinking all my troubles were over and I will be a professional LPN in twelve months. Surprisingly I was wrong.

Sheltered all my life living with my parents attended

segregated schools until moving in with Larry. I never experienced any form of oppression, not even on my jobs. In nursing school I was no longer living amongst peers, but a young black woman seeking a nursing career which was not very promising in a society where the majority of white nursing students out numbered the blacks students thirty to one. For the first time in my life I was entering a new dimension where I had never trampled before, a place that held prestige, power and knowledge. People like me was not openly accepted but confronted with racism, prejudice, and jealousy in the rawest form. It was a fact white people felt they were the superior race deserving better things in this world and blacks were the inferior race who for many years were oppressed and held back from getting what they rightfully deserved as a human race.

The black race deprived the right of an education since slavery is still being denied and blocked from academic success today. Education is a powerful tool that can change a person, a nation and the world. To emphasize obtaining a nursing degree was a challenge beyond my imagination with the mighty forces of evil against me like a mighty tide. Fear can paralyze the little faith anyone has resulting in the inability to fight the enemy. Reflecting back on the reasons I began this journey in the first place I had to fight. I had to fight to get off welfare. I had to fight to support my kids as a single mother. I had to fight so I wouldn't have to depend on a man. I had to fight for a job that would give me financial security. Trusting God with a made up mind I promised myself no matter what obstacles or challenges come across my path I was determined to make it remembering to hold steadfast to God's unchanging hands and he will not allow the enemy to destroy me only make me stronger. Nevertheless I became committed to rising to the full potential and purpose God had planned for my life.

~*Divine Inspiration: For this purpose was I born. When my life is for a purpose, I will rise above all difficulties.*~

The first day of class there were fifty female students enrolled in the class thirty-five whites and fifteen blacks all with the same aspirations and dream of becoming a nurse. None of us anticipated the struggles and challenges we were about to face on our new journey that was ahead of us. The Sea-Isle Vocational Center, an old elementary school was converted into a Adult Vocational Center. Our classroom was on the second floor with the old metal heaters that lined the walls and the brown and crème large square tiles floors, it was obvious the school was very old. The first quarter instructors were Mrs. Hendrix and Mrs. Lancaster who taught Vocational Relations, Geriatrics, Anatomy& Physiology, Skills, and Nutrition with Anatomy and Physiology.

The first quarter was held in the classroom setting consisted of comprehending large volumes of information. Learning concepts and theories along with comprehensive lecturing, taking notes was absolutely necessary. Reading on a college level was so different from reading in high school sometimes finding it very difficult to keep up with all the required reading. However making up my own methodology to assure the lecture material was retained in my brain cells enabled me to pass the exam by reading each chapter three times. During the long hours of reading I absorbed and dissected the information comprehending every single word of the text. Once the information was comprehended it became stored in my brain memory cells, therefore what ever question presented on the exam I was capable and competent to choose the correct answer. Keeping a medical and general dictionary available during my reading assignments to look up the meaning of unfamiliar words with this methodology I built the confidence needed to pass all my exams.

The brain is an amazing organ consisting of about one billion neurons, each forms about 1,000 connections to other neurons, amounting to more than a trillion connections. (Reber 2010). In memorization the logic or reasoning is eliminated however reading and comprehending retained information in my brain cells for a long period of time benefited me to passing exams. In anatomy and physiology we learned concepts and theories from an intense curriculum of comprehensive classroom lectures under the supervision and guidance of instructors to prepare us for the clinical environment was a challenge. As a result I sacrificed everything to pass the first quarter, coming home from school fixing my sons dinner, then hitting the books. Truly believing the extensive reading the chapters repeatedly paid off and my grade average remained 90-94%. But it was devastating to see ten students who were not able to maintain an 81% average eliminated from the program. It was hard to watch their faces full of despair and shame, too heartbroken to utter a single word due to the pain of failure. I was so grateful to have made it through by the grace of God using the methodology that seem to work for me.

Denise Richmond and I became the best of friends, nearly inseparable throughout the program sharing our struggles and fears during this difficult journey. Married with one daughter she worked in a nursing home as a nursing assistant often sharing how much she hated her job hoping to become a nurse through this program. Denise a highly emotional and

excitable person was very expressive with her facial over-
tones and whenever she was stressed or angry you knew it
by the expression on her face. Whereas I was completely the
opposite hiding my feelings and fears from the people around
me. Denise and I spent a lot of hours studying together focusing day and night on successfully passing the course. We
practically ate, slept, and drank nursing school with one goal
in mind completing this program doing whatever it took.

*~Divine Inspiration: "Put your hope in God." There is
never a time when we should not put our hope in God,
whatever our need or however difficulty our journey
before you may be. Even when the challenge appears to
be impossible our work is to hope in God.~*

The second quarter courses were Emergency Nursing,
Pharmacology, and Administration of Medications. Emergency
Nursing taught us how to provide nursing care for patients in
emergency, critical illness or severe injury. Nurses must be
trained to recognize quickly a life-threatening problem and
solve them on the spot. Most nurse interventions in an emergency situation are designed to stabilize the patient first, tend
to pain issue attempting to minimize the pain as much as possible, quickly uncover medical conditions and teach patient
about injury prevention. A nurses responsibility is to educate
patients about their conditions and what treatments are needed. Emergency Nursing is a great foundation course for students interested in becoming an Emergency Room nurse or
working in Intensive Care Units. What was so exciting about
this course everybody passed.

In Pharmacology we learned all about drugs, the generic
and trade names, categories, physiology and side effects the

drug had on various body systems. We were expected to learn dosages and possible interactions between medications for infants, children and adults. A nurse not properly trained in administering medications can put her patient's life at great risk. Pharmacology is one of the most difficult courses in nursing school and every student feared taking the course. Our instructor, Mrs. Nelms a middle age tall, thin black woman in her early fifties, developed a strong bond with the black students in our class. Taking us under her wings she mentored and coached us on how to become nurses. Mrs. Nelms the first black and highest paid pharmacology instructor in the Memphis City School System was battling with ovarian cancer had to fight daily for her life and job. Obviously she saw herself in us and wanted to see us succeed.

Surprisingly one day in the clinical classroom Mrs. Nelms made a covenant with all the black students in the class giving her word she would try to hold on as our instructor throughout the course before she retired. She said the word retired but we knew she really meant her death. To know she cared enough about us to do such a thing gave me reassurance and gratefulness. God sent an angel in our lives when we needed her the most. Mrs Nelms was always fair never treating the black students better than the white students and never making any student feel stupid or not good enough to become a nurse. We all successfully completed Pharmacology with the guidance and leadership of Mrs. Nelms prepared for Administration to Medications.

Divine Inspiration: Every valley that may arise, the difficult places encountered, let it sink in your inner being and rest your weary head and know, "This is my doing," says God.~

Administration of Medications teach nurses how to provide safe administration of medications by calculating dosages using the conversion factor and learning the five rights of administering medication is the foundation of giving medications safety. When administering medications, it is vital to remember the "Five Rights" of medication : 1) the right medication 2) the right dose 3) the right time 4) the right route 5) the right patient. The nurse should make sure the five rights are in place before giving her patient a medication will keep patient safe and free from harm. Mrs. Golden, the instructor, a middle aged white woman with a short, round plump figure, showed no passion for teaching and her attitude exemplified, "If you get it you do and if you don't oh well." Failing the very first exam I was devastated and overwhelmed leaving me confused losing all faith and not knowing what to do. The key and principle to calculating dosages was understanding the formulas. I spent hours every day working as many problems as I could over and over trying to learn how to master the concept. After finally beginning to understand the adult formulas we had to learn how to calculate dosages for the infant and child which was totally different from the adult formulas. Negative voices in my head kept saying, "Why don't you forget nursing school? Maybe this isn't the right field for you? You need to find something else to do." These negative voices playing over and over not allowing me to forget what I believed, I wasn't good enough to be a nurse.

Struggling the next morning to get out of bed I prayed, "Please God let this old 1972 blue and white Pinto make it until I finished school and O God please help me on my next Administration to Medication test." I wasn't alone, in fact, the whole class struggled knowing in our hearts there would be an enormous drop in the enrollment after this class. To emphasize having failed two exams my average wasn't looking very promising needing a 90 or higher on the final exam to pass the course. During the final exam fearful this would be the end for me began thinking how much depended on me passing this course. My dream career, my self-worth, my livelihood all could be over with just the matter of a few points. By the Grace of God I successfully passed with a 87 average. Unfortunately fifteen students were eliminated from the program failing to meet the 81% average to advance to the next quarter leaving only thirty-five students in the class. Denise a nervous wreck made it through barely and quit her job to focus completely on the program. Was nursing worth all this agony and pain?

Divine Inspiration: After blessings comes the battle. When our souls are caught in the Devil's grip, it is a trial that always end in victory for those who have committed the keeping of their souls to God.~

CHAPTER **9**

Enemy's Seed

THE THIRD QUARTER courses were Obstetrics, Pediatrics, and Mental Health and we were starting clinical rotations in a hospital setting learning to apply our classroom knowledge to actual patients. We performed nursing skills, administration of medication, giving intramuscular injections, and bedside nursing practice under the supervision of our instructor. All things considered this was a very new experience entering into a clinical setting in my nursing career. Little did I know the most horrific and racist act that changed my entire life would be projected on me a young black nursing student.

Obstetrics the care of the pregnant woman included; pre-conception period, pregnancy, labor and delivery, postpartum care, general health of the woman, care of her reproductive organs, breasts and sexual functions. Mrs. Jennings our instructor was a white middle age woman who had the perfect figure, her clothes fit perfect and extremely neat from head to toe. She had tall salt and pepper hair every string always in place. Her lectures were taught straight from the textbook. Using my methodology reading the chapters thoroughly over and over comprehending and storing the information in my brain cells passed everyone of her exams with scores 100, 99, 98. Surprisingly I couldn't understand why the white students were struggling with scores 40's and 65's. Granted if this was all I had to do it would have been glorious.

Denise made 98, 97, 99 on her exams too. I noticed there was a notably difference in how things were handled between the white and black students who persistently made low grades. The blacks were counseled and placed on probation even one was eliminated from the program, nevertheless the whites were not counseled. Such blatant forms of discrimination sparked an awareness in me how unfair instructors were when it came to black versus white nursing students. Whenever I passed Mrs. Jennings exam she would give me a vengeful and hostile look giving me the impression she did not care for me. Was it because I was smart? Or was it because I was black? All things considered I experienced a subtle form of prejudice and racism for the first time in my life, the beginning of being a vulnerable victim of racism and discrimination.

~Divine Inspiration: We often get into trouble when we try to walk by feelings rather than faith. At all times we must Trust God's word and His power more than we trust our feelings, beliefs, and experiences.~

Our clinical rotation were on days Tuesday and Thursday at Saint Francis Hospital in the Labor and Delivery Department. We were instructed to meet in the hospital lobby bright and early at 0645 in the mornings dressed and prepared for clinical. Arriving to the lobby Mrs. Jennings was already there, her body language was stand offish with arms folded across her chest, and nose in the air displaying such a high sense of superiority running through her veins that was extremely intimidating and threatening. My first clinical skill was the insertion of a foley catheter in a patient while in labor. This was my very first attempt inserting a Foley catheter so I expected her to assist and coach me through the procedure. Instead she stood at a distance watching with her arms folded without uttering a single word. All in all I proceeded to perform the skill, holding the patient left thigh with my left hand using my right hand to insert the catheter when she abruptly interrupted me saying, "You have contaminated the sterile field." Instantly freezing in my tracks not realizing exactly what I had done wrong. She quickly ordered me to find another skill to do. Humiliated I removed the dirty gloves walking away with my head down thinking it was all over for me.

It was obvious Mrs Jennings did not show any empathy that this was my first time ever attempting this skill. Meanwhile the not good enough addiction engulfed me as I wandered aimlessly searching the clinical area for another skill to do. I peered from a distance watching Mildred the white student nurse perform the same skill, contaminating the sterile field three times before finally inserting the catheter successful on the fourth try. I was enraged with anger. Driving home that evening angry, hurt, feeling rejected believed I wasn't t good enough to be a nurse. Fearfully knowing that my future lies in the hands of this vicious and cruel woman I wanted to give up. I wondered what would happen next in my career? Was it over? Are all my dreams gone down the drain? Will I have to go back to government assistance? These thoughts filled my mind causing fear to engulf my soul.

~Divine Inspiration: God tests our faith. True faith sustains us in the most trying of times, even when

everything around us seems to go against God's word.
Faith that believes will see.~

The next day filled with fear prayed fervently while sitting in my Ford Pinto like always before entering the school building. During class Mrs. Jennings made an announcement she needed to see me and Michelle after class. Michelle was another black student who struggled with her grades was put on probation if her average remained below 81% she would be eliminated from the nursing program. She informed me with no empathy or concern if I failed to insert a foley catheter properly during the next clinical day I will be eliminated from the nursing program placing me on probation too. Speechless feeling helpless finding it extremely hard to believe this was actually happening to me. Was my dream of becoming a nurse and independence coming to an end? Despite all the agony and pain she had dropped on me she added these very cold and nonchalant words "Maybe nursing is not for you and you should consider another profession." Those words felt like a dagger piercing my soul. I was distraught, hurt, humiliated finding it hard to believe this woman wanted to destroy me, destroy my future, destroy my life, destroy my dream. Leaving the room feeling crushed and hopeless, thinking all I wanted was to have a successful career, not have to depend on government assistance, be an independent woman, take care of my two boys and one day buy a home.

Mrs. Jennings seem to attack me in every way. Young and naive I didn't know how to fight back not realizing people could be so cruel in this world. Was she projecting such cruelty and meanness because I was passing all her classroom exams? Was she displeased with the fact this little black girl was smarter than the white girls? She was a satanic force attempting to plant her seed of defeat in me and I either had to accept this seed of defeat or to accept the seed of faith that if God is for me then who can be against me and no weapon formed against me shall prosper. I knew this scripture very well but my faith was weak.

~Divine Inspiration: "When the enemy comes in like a flood, know this is my doing, and your weakness needs my strength, and your safety lies in letting Me fight your battles," says God.~

There was no reprimanding or counseling given to Mildred after contaminating the sterile field three times while Michelle and I was counseled and both placed on probation. Inflamed with anger at the unfairness and prejudice projected by this instructor who threatened my livelihood and future I left school devastated, victimized, doubtful, afraid, and ashamed. Never facing anything so terrible in my life with all odds pointing against me I began to pray trying to remain strong in front of my sons while at the same time this horrific trial was suffocating the life out of me. In a valley of dismal and despair the Almighty God was the only one that could help me out of this trying and difficult time. I could not fight this devil alone. I began to pray like never before remembering I only needed faith the size of a mustard seed for God to move.

Weighed down with a heavy burden that my nursing career could possibly be over I tried not to let the pain show on my face in front of my boys and was relieved when they went outside to play. This reminded me of the Jews in the book of Esther awaiting their destiny after hearing the decree all the Jews would be annihilated in eight months. Can you imagine the agony these people had to endure when their fate rested in the hands of a cruel official of the king. Feeling similar pain and agony with only one day awaiting, this instructor wanted to annihilate me from the nursing program. Sitting down at my dining room table I pulled out my skills and procedure book turning to the chapter on, "How To Insert a Foley Catheter." I began reading the entire chapter one page at a time absorbing every word into my brains cells.Then I read the chapter a second time and a third time until I felt confident and prepared to insert a foley catheter without contaminating the sterile field. Barely able to sleep tossing over and over in my mind how will things will unfold on tomorrow?

The next day in clinical Mrs. Jennings instructed me to prepare to insert the foley. Feeling confident gathered all of my supplies proceeded to explain and educate the patient what was about to happen. Then professionally applied the knowledge retained by inserting the foley catheter with dexterity and execution competently without contaminating the sterile field. After the catheter was inserted in the bladder, observing the flow of urine through the tubing confirmed the placement of the catheter. I waited but I didn't hear those dreadful words, "You have contaminated the sterile field," I knew I had made it through. I don't think I will ever forget how to insert a Foley catheter even if I tried. God uses trials to make us stronger to prepare us for what he has for us in the future.

~*Divine Inspiration: "They intended to harm me, but God intended it for my good to accomplish what is now being done." Genesis 50:20.*~

Mrs. Jennings standing with her arms fold never uttered

one word of approval or satisfaction out of her mouth with a look of disgust on her face as she turned and walked away. With a load lifted from my shoulders I was grateful to the Almighty God for allowing me to come out victorious passing this course with 87(B) final grade.

In the third quarter Pediatrics the study and care of infants, children and adolescence we learned concepts, theories, with a clinical practicum providing real-life experiences applying the knowledge to practice. In addition to learning multiple and complex needs of children we also learned to interact with staff and other healthcare personnel which can be very stressful for a student. The purpose of clinical is to get the student familial with the patient care and hospital environment as much as possible. This clinical rotation took place in a doctors' officer and we learned to write nursing care plans which requires a lot of research and writing. A care plan is a very important intrinsic aspect of the nursing process which outline the plan of action according to the diagnosis given by the doctor to be implemented during a patients' medical care. Writing care plans are complex and complicated but an important aspect of the nursing process. My clinical experience in pediatric nursing caring was enjoyable but this wasn't where my heart desired to work. My study methodology reading, studying, and comprehending the chapters three times did not let up and continued to pass my exams. I passed this course with a score of 91B.

In Mental Health Nursing we learn how to care for mentally ill patients, which is one of the most complex areas of study in nursing school ever encountered other than Administrations to Medications. One of the most important attribute required in mental health nursing is learning the capability to develop and form a therapeutic relationship with patients and their families while listening and interpreting their needs and concerns. The appropriate response is so critical. Using a range of cognitive behavioral therapy skills while communicating is essential when providing care for these type patients to recover their mental health so they can live to their fullest potential. All the multiple choice exams were challenging and difficult to choose with all the questions focusing on how to relate to a mentally ill patient. If you understand the mental health diagnosis of the patient, your chances of choosing the correct answer were better. Throughout nursing school students heard all the time, 'There are always two correct answers but you will need to choose the best answer.' I could accept this analogy with the other nursing courses to choose the correct intervention, or correct information from the textbook, but in Mental Health it was difficult to choose the appropriate response to a mentally ill patient. Continuing to apply my methodology, reading the chapters two and three times and studying my notes over and over again until the material was instilled in my brain cells surprisingly passed the course with a grade 87 B. Our class attendance dropped from 25 to 14 students at the end of this course.

~Divine Inspiration: Without faith it is impossible to please God. Whenever God reveals something He expects us to believe Him and adjust our lives accordingly Hebrews 11:6.~

CHAPTER 10

Rejected But Not Denied!

IN OUR LAST quarter we studied Diet Therapy and Medical Surgery. In Diet Therapy Mrs. Golden taught the major nutrients, good health, proper diet for patients, and the importance of the four basic food groups. Diet Therapy made a major impact in my life learning essential facts about food and nutrients, the body physiology and how it functions and how it's sustained by food. When it comes to the body if we eat a healthy balanced meal eighty percent of the time we earn the right to eat what we want twenty percent of the time, called the 80/20 rule. The body an amazing creation by God is our temple and where the Holy Spirit dwells and we should always be mindful of how we treat it. The entire class passed with flying colors and my grade was 94 A.

Our last course Medical Surgery Mrs. Marlowe our instructor taught how to relate normal body functions to pathological changes caused by a disease process. Mrs. Marlowe a tall obese white woman with dirty blonde hair that always appeared unkept. Denise and I did exceptionally well on the classroom exams which wasn't the problem. In the clinical setting there were no pass or fail grade, instead an evaluation and assessment of your performance skills by the instructor who decides whether your performance was satisfactory or unsatisfactory. After experiencing a traumatic experience last semester I worked aggressively and extremely hard striving to make a satisfaction on my clinical performance hoping and praying this would not happen again.

Our clinical rotation took place at Baptist Memorial Hospital downtown on a very busy Med-Surgical Unit consisting of 50 patients. The two days of clinical was usually fast paced trying to memorize our drugs, taking care of our patients and not leave anything undone. During evaluation Denise received an unsatisfactory on her performance and she was outraged. Her body language expressed her anger with her rolling of eyes, sticking our her lip, arms folded and turning to walk in the opposite direction whenever she saw Mrs. Marlowe. The following week Mrs. Marlowe eliminated Denise from the program for charting incorrectly on a deceased patient. Deborah was petrified. I was petrified. How could she do this to Denise a student learning how to chart on an incident of this magnitude? The whole class was shocked Mrs. Marlowe was so unfair toward Denise eliminating her from the program. Denise so devastated in a state of shock was speechless with hopelessness shown all over her face. Lost for words I didn't know how to console my friend. She had invested so much into this program, quitting her job and for eleven long months studying relentlessly with fear constantly held over her head. What she had feared most had come upon her.

~Divine Inspiration: Fear is faith turned inside out and does not come from God, but causes us to question Him. God gives us a sound mind to see things clearly. He

gives us the Holy Spirit so we are able to see things as He sees them.~

There was a young lady in our class name Carin who was very knowledgeable and outspoken. This was Carin second time through the program and she was always giving us tidbits of wisdom and advice. When she heard the news about Denise she immediately notified Mrs. Nelms our Pharmacology instructor who had resigned after teaching our class due to the progression of her cancer but fulfilled her promise to see our class through Pharmacology. Although Mrs. Nelms were deathly sick with cancer we still could count on her. She contacted Mrs Shirley Brown, the superintendent over the vocational department who happened to be a black woman informing her of the injustice carried out by Mrs. Marlowe. Mrs. Brown arranged a meeting to be held at the hospital with Mrs. Marlowe, Mrs. Brown and Denise. While the meeting was held in a small room on the unit all the students waited anxiously in the halls to see what the outcome would be.

After approximate 45 minutes Denise exited the room with a smile all over her face we knew the outcome. She was reinstated back into the program and Mrs. Marlowe was placed on probation. Hallelujah God is Good! Denise shared some of the things said in the meeting and the one thing that stood out the most was when Mrs. Brown told Mrs. Marlowe she was a student nurse once too, and she didn't know how to chart on a deceased patient correctly the very first time either. There were only eleven students remaining in our class for graduation, five blacks and six whites with the privilege to march down the aisle on December 17, 1987 at 7:00 p.m. on Friday night. Denise recited the speech "Don't Quit" victoriously with so much zeal facing the auditorium filled with family and friends. Mrs. Nelms a true mentor was only in our lives for a season, all in all it was during a difficult time during my nursing career. She shared her knowledge and wisdom freely through her unconditional love, support and lessons that opened our hearts to learning how to become professional nurses. I will always remember her as an angel God sent down from heaven for only a season and I will never forget her.

After graduation we all gathered in the lobby with our families and friends to celebrate this glorious occasion. Isn't it true that our joys are made better when sorrows are in the midst of them. Even though Denise had reached the pit of her valley, in the center of all her sorrows her walk appeared seemingly hopeless, when God stretched out His hand against the anger of her foes. He will bring our trouble to completion, causing the enemy's' attacks to fail. Driving home I thought, "I made it. Almighty God who directed my steps made a way out of no way." A peace came over me knowing that God's hand was behind every satanic attack that came against me. Truly elated and filled with joy I was glad it was over and now I could start a new life. Completing nursing school certainly was the greatest accomplishment second to having my two sons. Thankful and grateful I knew it was nothing but the grace of God who made both happen.

~Divine Inspiration: I can do all things through Christ who gives Me strength Philippians 4:13. These trials will show that your faith is genuine 1 Peter 1:7.~

CHAPTER 11

Rising Of Faith

MY FAITH AND confidence in God begin to rise to a new level drawing me closer to Him believing He called me for His purpose. I began to delight myself in the Lord, saying yes to him, walking in faith and accomplishing great things. In other words without God my abilities are dreams without power. God lets me know, no matter what happens, He offers me hope and promise even when the enemy come against me at all corners of my world. God allowed all my adversities to happen because His plans for me is not for me to under-stand why certain things happen but to trust in Him. He al-lowed oppositions for my good making me stronger for what I would have to face in the future. His plan is for me to grow closer to Him and maintain a relationship holding on with one little finger of faith and that would be enough to make it. There were times when I asked, "Where is God? Why is He allowing the enemy to come against me ?" Now I realize He was right there providing His mercy and grace allowing only what he allowed to happen. God never said he would save me from trouble because this is a fallen world, and adversity will come my way. God knew in order for me to survive and become successful in my career as a nurse I must endure trials and tests pruning and molding me into the image more like Christ. He would provide me with the wisdom to cope, strength to conquer my problems, and trust in Him, and that was all I needed.

~Divine Inspiration: "When you go through deep waters I will be with you. When you go through rivers of difficulty, you will not drown. When you walk through the fire of oppression, you will not be burned up; the flames will not consume you." Isaiah 43:2~

Nonetheless completing nursing school is a great accomplishment and a joyous moment in my life however at the same time emotionally crippled from the shame, rejection, humiliation, and intimidation projected onto me. A statement made so cold by instructor Mrs. Jennings effected my self-esteem in such a profound way when she uttered those dreadful words, "Nursing is not for you and you should consider another career besides nursing." Then she placed me on probation. These words still rang in my ears as if they were just spoken, thinking about it constantly not realizing the enormous weight words carry that can effect a person life for decades.

~Divine Inspiration: What so a man thinketh so is he. Proverbs 23:7~

In fact research has shown that negative words setbacks is three times powerful than positive progress. It's just easier to remember negative stuff than positive. Our brains are wired to pay attention to negative experiences as a protective device, scanning for threats. God and His creation is amazing.

~Divine Inspiration: Death and life are in the power of the tongue. Proverbs 18:21~

Notably a young lady, very shy suffering from low self-esteem, a not good enough addiction and lack of confidence allowed what people said and thought effect my life's decisions. Feeling trapped inside my own body unable to do what I wanted but instead what people expected. My life colored with low self-esteem, not good enough, and lack of self-worth restricted me in every aspect of my life revealing fear and weakness. Surrounded by people and situations that never saw me for who I am, wrestled with not being accepted, people pleasing, rejection and denial. Instead of love, support and encouragement, remembered criticism and rejection leading to poor choices that interfered with having a healthy mature life. No matter what our race or what other people think or say about us, the first limitations we must overcome are those we place on ourselves. Self-esteem is a value we all need as a human being but for women it is a distinguishing quality stemming from the way we are raised and any discrimination or inferior treatment makes us vulnerable later in life. Even after my brilliant achievement I continued to wrestle with low self esteem and not standing up for what was rightfully mind.

All through the program I suffered with a fear of the not being good enough addiction even though I could hear God saying, "Do not have a spirit of fear but of sound mind." A voice in my mind kept saying otherwise, 'You are not going to make it. You are going to have to remain on welfare. You need to choose another career. You are not nursing material.' Despite all my trials and tribulations my faith began to rise and I aspired nothing else but to be a nurse. I wanted to be a nurse so bad I could taste it. I prayed, read my bible, and developed a relationship with God realizing I needed Him and I could not fight the enemy alone.

With all the suffering endured through nursing school understood why God allows suffering in the world. Suffering brings us closer to Him. If there were no suffering we would never come to Him.

~Divine Inspiration: "I consider everything a loss compared to the surpassing greatness of knowing Christ Jesus my Lord Philippians 3:8~

We tend to feel we are doing the greatest good in the world when we are strong and fit and when our hearts and hands are busy with kind acts of service. But if we are patient and submissive to God it is almost certain we will be a greater blessing to the world around us during our time of suffering and pain than we were when we thought we were doing our greatest work.

CHAPTER 12

The Exam

AT GRADUATION WE were given temporary license permits until state board examinations were taken to receive our permanent license. However it was a pleasure to hold that little temporary paper in my hands that looked more like a receipt than a license. It validated in any case who I had become, a nurse. I made it through all the agony, pain and persecution that came along with becoming a nurse. Now having gone through the trenches I began preparing for the state board examination as soon as possible. I was never more serious about anything in my life, determined to pass the first time. The NCLEX-PN, National Council Licensure Examination, a standardized exam developed to assess a graduates' knowledge and competency to practice nursing. For the purpose of passing state boards exam reading everything was crucial. I read every textbook, lecture notes, and NCLEX-PN study guides, even buying a second NCLEX-PN study guide reviewing all the questions and answers placing emphasis on the rationale. The rationale usually found after the correct answer explains the educational purpose of the curriculum expressing the understanding of the question answer. Its purpose is to convince the importance of the proposed answer to the questions and explains why the answer is the best answer to the question .

Preparation for state board exam was emotionally draining and psychologically exhausting consuming my whole life. Denise and I studied relentlessly constantly quizzing each other with questions. Our trip together to Nashville on the bus were continued with quizzing, in the hotel room we quizzed each other until late into the night falling asleep holding our books in our arms. In order to achieve whatever you desire it takes a driven iron will, determination and effortless hard work planning for obstacles before they happen. Arriving the next morning to the testing center located in a large room appearing to be an old gymnasium with long tables lined up parallel to one another all over as far as I could see, I thought this is it. The test coordinators seated four students to each table preventing any room for cheating or wandering eyes. Overwhelmed with anxiety I watched the coordinators passing out the test booklets, all appearing to move in slow motion. I was more than ready to begin the exam and get this over with. I was set on go. Praying to myself, "You can do it. Read each question thoroughly and remember every question has two answers but you must choose the best answer."

~Divine Inspiration: Too often we settle for less than what God wants to do through us. "I am the Lord the God of all flesh. Is anything too hard for Me." Jeremiah 32:7~

However this was the most intimidating thing I've ever done in my whole life with so much depending on my passing, in contrast, prior to starting nursing school I was living a nonproductive life on welfare.

The examination consisting of 200 comprehensive multiple choice questions is designed to assess nursing students competence, skill and judgment. How much nursing knowledge retained from the course determines if you successfully passed the exam. The exam is designed to allow students every possible chance to pass if they studied and comprehended what they were taught. Nine out of ten times failure is if the student did not study correctly. Regardless people say they are not good test takers experiencing freezing up, mental blocks, racing thoughts, or difficulty concentrating. An exam of this magnitude will cause anxiety and stress to some of the most organized and prepared individuals no matter how much they have studied. Even after studying several NCLEX-PN study guides answering all the questions in the chapters, reading all my lecture notes, I still struggled pathetically with some of the multiple choice questions doubting if I had chose the correct answer. In a situation like this you have to believe in yourself, do your very best and trust God.

So close to my dream the voice of the not good enough spirit continued to tell me, "You still are not going to make it to the finish line. I told you to get out long time ago. You are not nursing material." This battle in my mind continued torturing me to no end. I prayed to God to help me fight this negative voice in my mind. I begin to wonder would a loving God bring me this close and abandon me now. Even though not committed to having a relationship with God I still cried out to him in a time of need. I was desperate and if failed I would be devastated. I knew several women who failed state board exam and still remember the hurt and disappointment in their eyes. They wore a wounded look on their faces and never had the courage to retake the exam allowing resentment to settle in their hearts. Whereas there was one lady whom I will never forget who failed six times but with determination, commitment and dedication refused to give up and finally passed. In essence with persistence, perseverance and faith there is always the opportunity to pass. Why would anyone invest so much of their time and energy completing a nursing program give and not try again until they passed. Having gone through a nursing program, the training, the emotionally and psychological stress is remembered the rest of your life. The key word here is persistence in your books and notes steadfastly and firmly in some state, purpose, course of action to endure tenaciously to succeed.

After the first session of the exam it was a relief to come up for air. A test of this magnitude consumes your whole mind body and soul that weighed on my heart. We were given a hour for break to mingled in the halls and every face I looked upon there was so much doubt, fear and unbelief, nobody speaking a word. Was anybody holding on to God's hand through all of this? God was using everything to further His purpose in my life. I had to believe and hold on to God's unchanging hands. Then I begin reflecting on my life as a young girl when I watched my mother worked diligently as a cook, maid, and housekeeper six days a week then come home and stand all day in the kitchen. This was another reason I had to succeed it. I wanted to be more.

Denise was a nervous wreck, speechless shaking her head as we looked at each other in awe. At this point the not good enough voice told me, "There is no way you passed that first half of that test." I was saturated with uncertainty over the questions I was doubtful about running rampant through my brain over and over. I read on the internet that no matter how well a student performed on state board exams they still feel they performed poorly. I called on God to break through my fears and calm my heart remembering what we've all heard He will never give us more than we can bear. The fact I had completed the program enduring trials and tribulations is a testimony to my strength and will to survive refusing to give up like so many women had. I wanted to be a nurse overcoming the not good enough voice and go after my dream with all my heart. After the second session of the exam the doubt consumed me with my faith and trust going out the window. My faith wasn't strong enough. I didn't have enough of God's Word in me. Faith is built on hearing the word over and over. Why was I putting so many limitations on my faith? Hadn't God already shown me what he can do in my life? Didn't he allow me to pass through the nursing program? When I can't FAITH can.

~Divine Inspiration: When great challenges come before me, my first impulse is to give up and sit down in despair amid my dashed hopes. But the scripture says, " Faith is the confidence that what we hope will actually happen." Hebrews 11:1~

On the bus back Denise and I quizzed each other all the way back to Memphis. We were filled with doubt trying to remember as many questions as possible to see if we chose the same answers. There was no advanced technology with computerized testing so we had to wait four to six weeks for our results in the mail. It was nerve wrenching and shameful students had to wait this long to get results after wrecking their brains during the exam. Back home trying to keep my mind off my exam results start looking for a job holding onto that slip of paper, my temporary permit, with so much pride. Deep down I was very proud of what I had accomplished hoping I was on my way to having a successful career with financial security living as an independent woman. I never want to rely on government assistance or a man again but only God who supplies all my needs if I trust and put Him first in my life.

~Divine Inspiration: Work hard and become a leader;
be lazy and become a slave.Proverbs 22:29~

CHAPTER **13**

First Nurse Job

I WAITED ANXIOUSLY on my exam results watching intently for the mail carrier to put mail in my box everyday praying my results is passing. Finally receiving a long write envelope from Tennessee State Board of Nursing my heart began to race with sweat oozing from every pore as I frantically tore the envelop until I saw bold letters in the top right corner that read **PASSED**. I threw the letter in the air singing Hallelujah dancing all through my apartment thanking God Almighty for his goodness. Indeed a great burden was lifted and now I could concentrate on moving forward with my life knowing in my heart it was my destiny to be a nurse.

My job hunting didn't go so well, every place I applied they wanted someone with experience. How was I suppose to have experience when I just got out of school? I became discouraged remembering the rumors all through nursing school, " LPNs were no longer going to be hired in hospitals and medical facilities, and they were going to fade out." Even though these thoughts lingered in my head, I tried to have an optimistic view, never believing everything I hear, continued looking for a job hoping to find something soon.

At the time hospitals were hiring more registered nurses, particularly those with a bachelor's degree with goals of becoming Magnet status facilities, with fewer and fewer LPNs being hired. Magnet status is awarded by the American Nurses' Credentialing Center (ANCC) to hospitals that meet certain criteria related to the quality of nursing care.

~Divine Inspiration: You must keep faith alive in your life created by your experiences you encounter, always seeking to broaden your horizons to go higher than where you are at the moment becoming more faithful.~

Searching for a job tirelessly until responding to an ad in the newspaper from Nursing Personnel Pool, an independent employer. They were devoted to supplying skilled, trained nurses in various hospitals, nursing homes, and clinics providing staffing needs. Surprisingly I was hired the same day after successfully passing a pharmacology exam. I was sent on an assignment the next day at Methodist Central Hospital working thirty-two hours a week on the 3-11 shift. I was so grateful to have my first nursing job and thrilled to be making more money than ever before in my life. Agency nurses are paid higher hourly rates than regular staff because they are paid no benefits or insurance. Hospitals spends an enormous amount of money paying for agency nurses and over the years have tried to do away with hiring agency staff due to the higher hourly rates but with the nursing shortage that is difficult to do. There are advantages and disadvantages working for an agency. The advantages are hourly rates are higher and you can get your pay weekly. The disadvantages are there are no benefits, no insurance, no guarantee shifts your work depending on the census each day. However with the nursing shortages I was never called off but able to get all the shifts I wanted including overtime. God Is Good!

~Divine Inspiration: Do not be surprised if your answer comes through the doors closed allowing God to open the right one after submitting your request.~

As a LPN I worked in the hospital providing basic bedside nursing care under the supervision of a registered nurse and doctors. Some of my nursing duties were; vital signs, head-to-toe physical assessments, charting, carrying out physicians orders, injections, enemas, insert foley catheters, dress wounds, IV therapy, insertion of IVs, entering orders in the computers, assisted with bathing, dressing and personal hygiene, turning patient every two hours to prevent bedsores, assistance to bathrooms, and assistance with ambulation. Sometimes the job responsibilities of the registered nurse and practical nurse can be the same and often overlap. Many practical nurses have a problem being supervised by a registered nurse causing friction and resentment on the job but this only inspired me to go back to school. God gives each of us the same opportunities in life, we just have to reach for the prize. Our true commitment is how we respond to the opportunity we have been given. Will we increase the talent and multiply it or will we sit on it or bury it and never use it for God's purpose?

Nursing homes assignments allowed one nurse to have 16-18 patients and when short staff that number would double. The LPN's primary role is to care for the elderly; making sure they maintain acceptable personal hygiene, clean linens, proper nutrition, medication administration, each patient having ten or more medications scheduled. Sometimes a medication nurse and treatment nurse were staffed in order to get all the patient care done in 24 hours. The nursing assistants did the personal care, preparing the patient for meals, getting patient out the bed, and keeping their room clean. Nursing homes are very busy with a tremendous workload, nurses rushing from room to room making it almost impossible to attend to all of her patients needs.

~Divine Inspiration: Going forward I am committing, affirming, supporting and staying focused on my goals.~

CHAPTER 14

First Home

AFTER WORKING FULL time for six months passionately and diligently I contacted a real estate agency to discuss the possibility of purchasing my first home having saved nearly three thousand dollars in my bank account. Currently living in a newly renovated apartment, under Section 8, a government assisted program which helped women on welfare find decent housing, with $0 monthly rent and receiving a subsidized check for the utilities I realized I was already blessed. Praises Go Up. God Is Good! Now on my job for six months feeling emotionally and financially stable I decided to move forward purchasing my first house. I soon learned anything worth having, doesn't come easy and buying a new home takes stamina, commitment and a desire to navigate through the time consuming process . I believed if I took one step forward God is going to take two steps. All in all the process can get confusing and even overwhelming trying to weigh all the options and making the best decisions came with long sleepless nights.

Sometimes leaving the familiar and embracing the unknown is frightening but I knew in order for me to grow, to follow my dream, no matter how difficult the challenge, change is necessary. I am a fighter and determined to pursue my life dream of having my own home. After I watched my mother's dream of having her own home go down the drain I promised myself I would not let this happen to me. My father a G.I.Veteran qualified him to pay only one dollar down on a brand new home, but he never took advantage of the opportunity. The American dream didn't interest him. His whole life centered around working two jobs, spending all of his leisure time at his favorite club Sam's Lounge. Meanwhile my mother became bitter and resentful never getting her the house every woman dream of owning one day. She made degrading remarks he was no good and didn't have anything and didn't want anything. I actually thought she hated my daddy. My mother never had the opportunity to buy her own home worked as a maid in a private home for senior citizens for over 30 years making just enough to make ends meet.

~Divine Inspiration: Strains, struggle, frustration, tension, anxiety, compulsion, obsession and fear are the results we get when we are pushing to hard and not correctly aligned with God. God doesn't have to push to get us what we want.~

After a week of house shopping it wasn't hard to find the perfect little two bedroom brick house in the heart of Whitehaven built in 1955 by a little white elderly couple who still resided in the home. The real estate agent took me touring through the house taking along Bernard and Monterio. It was obvious the house was very well kept and in good condition and I fell in love with it. I began to work double shifts to pay for the extra expenses, pay off delinquent creditors and everything possible to get my mortgage loan approved. It pays to keep your credit ratings good. I learned good credit is better than money in the bank. The journey of success isn't easy and people are going to throw stones but I learned how to turn some of those stones into milestones and keep going forward. The battle never ends and with God in the mist, He will fight my battles when I get out the way, because I can't fight the enemy. All in all becoming a new homeowner was one of the most exhilarating moments of my life. Bernard wasn't too happy about leaving all his friends behind and starting over at a new school. Monterio was a mommas boy, it didn't seem to matter which way the wind blew for him. Being a homeowner and a single mother trying to juggle a full-time job and full-time parenting can seem impossible but with God and determination it is possible. Owning my home is one of the best financial investment I could of made. Living under Section 8 program there were so many stipulations, but with my own home I had the freedom to paint my walls any color I please or change all the draperies in each room. There is a certain pride that comes with owning your own home that I didn't understand being a renter.

~Divine Inspiration: Do you wonder why you are experiencing some great trials and tests? As your life unfolds God will always provide discipline you need when the next trial comes your way in the future as your faith grows.~

CHAPTER **15**

Enemy Within

WORKING FOR NURSING Personnel Pool nine months with enough experience under my belt I decided to apply for a job at Baptist Minor Medical Center, a small clinic located in the Whitehaven area, operated by one medical doctor and LPNs. I gained knowledge and experience in a variety of nursing skills not performed in the hospital such as; drawing blood, x-rays, splinting limbs, performing pap smears, EKGs, eye irrigations, physical examinations, gynecological pap smears, drug screens, and reading under the microscope. These skills developed competence in me as a new nurse and has remained with me throughout my nursing career.

A single mom who endured psychological and racial discrimination beat the odds of nursing school and buying a home for the first time, my self esteem begin to blossom to a new level. I no longer depended on welfare or a man to support me and my two sons. I was making good money and finally had reached a point in my life where I actually liked my life. I had accomplished two major accomplishments; finished nursing school and buying my first home. But life has a way of knocking you down if you take your eyes off your

Sovereign God and don't put him first in your life. He definitely has a way of getting your attention and putting you on your knees humbling you in the perfect school of humility where lessons are taught. He places our circumstances and the people around us only to accomplish His will. When we don't put Him first the devil makes room to reel his ugly head up in our life. Without a church home to belong to, nor reading my bible on a regular basis I didn't have a relationship with God, but I loved God and was grateful for what He had already done in my life.

~Divine Inspiration: There is a Divine Source, Powerful Force, a Perfect Order that controls everything. When we surrender and recognize this we won't have to struggle any longer.~

One day at work in the clinic a patient complaining of respiratory infection and a persistent cough came in. Dr Williams ordered 5cc cough syrup with codeine a narcotic controlled substance. After medicating the patient, the Tiger in me, the old self compelled me to do the unthinkable. The old self engulfed me. I poured myself 5cc of the the medication before placing it back in the narcotics cabinet. My past had come back to haunt me, enticing me to take the drug. Craving the euphoria and altered mood I remembered from my past of using alcohol and marijuana compelled me to do the unthinkable. Believing the Tiger in me was dead but realized it was only tamed I took the cough suppressant with codeine. The Tiger became satisfied reaching a feeling of euphoria feeling happier, more confident, relaxed, less self-conscious, bolder, and more talkative. Currently on a prescribed medication Flagyl to treat infection, not realizing the two drugs were contraindicated caused a severe drug reaction. Experiencing severe ataxia, jerky and involuntary movements in my arms and legs made it very difficult for me to walk without holding on to the wall. When Bernard saw this he was petrified with fear running to the phone to call my mother. I convinced them to please let me sleep. I prayed to God fervently that when this medicine cleared out my system I would never take another drug again.

~Divine Inspiration: The spirit is willing, but the flesh is weak. Matthews 26:41. When fearful turn to the spirit inside who is always guiding, protecting, loving to ensure we do our best.~

After working at the Baptist Minor Medical Center six months I was transferred to the new clinic opening on Poplar. This was a brand new clinic so I thought it would be nice to work in a brand new building. It was a much longer drive for me but working in a the nice building made up for that. The supervisor Sharon Blue LPN, a slender tall blonde in her late thirties or early forties had long stingy blonde hair. She wasn't very friendly toward me from day one expressing it through her voice and body language. The only black nurse at this location sensed this would become a problem. After working only two weeks, a former classmate, Mildred from nursing school was hired. Asking God "Do you have to keep putting these hard trials before me?" Reflecting back to that dreadful clinical day when I was put on probation for inserting a foley catheter incorrectly, Mildred was allowed three chances before she was successful and never reprimanded. This event still lingered in my mind, suffering from this humiliating and devastating experience I carried a lot of shame, resentment, and bitterness toward the instructor and Mildred as well. Feeling paranoid and still carrying shame inside about the situation wondered would she share this humiliating story with the people on the job. I tried to forget the agonizing and hurtful past and shrink into greatness, instead I continued to beat myself up with self criticism, judging, and condemnation more than the world could or would. I did not understand that my past simply told me what I can do, cannot do, what I need to work on to become better. I had to accept who I am and take the appropriate steps toward healing and correction.

Mildred a tall obese white woman was clumsy but intelligent, very manipulative, know-it-all and opinionated about everything. Not trusting her as far as I could see her there was always discord and opposition whenever we worked together. She took every opportunity to make me appear incompetent and I realized she was out to destroy my character and integrity in front of other co-workers. Always conducting myself as a professional loving and compassionate nurse realized my best qualities are only seen by the people who doesn't feel threatened or intimidated by my success. I was learning people don't hate you for your weaknesses, they hate you for your strengths. Working in a hostile environment disliked and unaccepted is what Mrs. Nelms had warned me about. I didn't t know how to fight the enemy. I had never experienced being attacked for who I am.

~Divine Inspiration: Wounds from a friend can be trusted, but an enemy multiplies kisses. Proverbs 27:6~

Desiring to be more and no longer settling for being a single mother living on welfare submitting to an abusive relationship I realized I was a Divine Child of God. I was not my name, job, or level of education. I was not who my mother, father, sister, husband, children say I am. I am who God say I am. To know me I had to love and accept me as a Divine Child of God having no excuse to be anything else for anyone else other than the Divine Father. I had a lot to learn on this journey of becoming better. Struggling to prove myself as a nurse I was challenged, insulted and intimidated every single day. Being the only black nurse no matter how professional, skilled or competent my work performances were it was never good enough or appreciated. Being a beautiful black and intelligent woman which didn't sit well with them there was attack after attack followed with discord, strife, jealousy and disagreements. I was weighed down with unfair treatment.

~Divine Inspiration: God never sends you into a situation alone. He will always precede you. He stands besides you, to provide protection and comfort. Psalms 139:7-12

With my six months evaluation the supervisor read off multiple complaints and write ups regarding my work performance even saying the doctors found it difficult to work with me. I sat listening to the lies finding it hard to believe the words coming out her mouth. Overall, this poor evaluation was nothing I had anticipated believing this was a conspiracy to get rid of me. Deep down I knew my job performance was satisfactory. I was an excellent nurse, but when you are hated in an hostile environment the devil over rules. Feeling rejected and frightened I sat silently hoping for an opportunity to improve my performance, when she proceeded to say "I'm going to have to fire you." Paralyzed in my chair with disillusionment I thought, 'How could she so easily just fire me like this. Didn't she know this is my livelihood, my career I had sacrificed so much for? My career that was just beginning.

~Divine Inspiration: Jesus is my perfect security in the storms of life. He has never promised me an easy road, only a safe landing.

Never given a proper warning according to policy I wasn't meeting standards expectations this came as a complete shock. Pulling up from the chair with all the strength I had left in my body keeping my head down refusing to look at this Devil I slowly left her office. I gathered all my things in my arms and left the facility. Driving home I thought how was I going to make ends meet having recently purchased a home for me and my two boys. I found myself sinking in the sands of doubt and fear praying, "Oh God, I don't want to go back on welfare. " In this spiritual warfare I felt they had won the battle. But I didn't understand at the time God had chosen me and the enemy attacks were allowed by God and He will never allow more than I can handle. When God's Chosen Ones are attacked the enemy sees and knows the spirit of God. Not equipped with the shield of faith, the Word of God, Satan can defeat and whip you. God allows humiliation, rejection to draw us closer to him.

CHAPTER **16**

Night Shift

I BEGAN SEARCHING for a new job immediately and got hired at Methodist South Hospital on February 28, 1989 after successfully passing a pharmacology test. Reflecting back to the Administration to Medications and Pharmacology in nursing school remembering how I wrecked my brain studying those math formulas and drugs. Thinking about sweet Mrs. Nelms whom I will hold dear in my heart forever taught me education really is not free, that it is so important, and I would have to fight to get it. She instilled courage and motivation in me that placed a fire in my spirit to make it through school whatever it took. The pharmacology test for the job couldn't compare to the stress and agony experienced in nursing school.

The sole purpose of requesting the 11-7 shift was to be home when my sons went to school and arrived back home, otherwise who wants to work what is better known as the graveyard shift. Bernard was twelve, very defiant and rebellious in and out of trouble was challenging and stressful. Monterio was six and the perfect kid who went to school every day, came home watched television, making the Honor

Roll every six weeks. What more could a mother ask? With no man in the house raising two boys alone was difficult and sometimes I thought I would lose my mind. I wasn't sure about leaving them home alone so I contacted Juvenile Court Department to ask if was it legal to leave my twelve year old and a six year home alone? They informed me if my twelve year old was competent and had no mental problems it would be appropriate.

Starting at Methodist South on the 3rd floor a medical-surgical unit I was excited to be working in a hospital that offered me benefits and insurance. My orientation preceptor was Sharon Valley, a white middle aged registered nurse with many years of nursing experience under her belt had a very nonchalant attitude. If I wanted to know something I had to ask. I was very observant watching everything closely determined to learn as much as I could, finding out I was on my own. There was a black LPN, Sherry Powell with 14 years experience who taught me the scoop on how things were really done. Currently in nursing school for her RN degree shared how many times she stopped and started her career. We became good friends working together for many years.

After my day shift orientation I was transferred to night shift. There I met my preceptor Joan Stringfield RN, a middle age white woman with eight years of nursing experience. Joan was the nicest white woman I had ever met who exemplified professionalism and excellent work ethics. She wore starched white uniforms and spotless white shoes every single night she came to work. As I watched her go in the patients' rooms her personality was so genuine and kind to every patient she interacted with calling them "hon" short for honey. She was patient and kind toward me making it comfortable to approach her anytime I needed help. This was priceless to have such an excellent preceptor who taught me something so valuable in the workforce, high moral work ethics that encompasses a positive and productive approach to professional nursing. According to the Tennessee Board of Nursing the job responsibilities between LPN and Registered Nurses vary state to state. LPNs are not allowed to work in specialty areas like the ER, ICU, NICU; but highly qualified to work in sub-acute areas in the hospitals, nursing homes, and in physician's offices. They are not allowed to perform physical assessments without an RN overseer. LPNs are not allowed to hang blood products or administer medication via intravenously.

On 3South nursing unit is where I became a nurse. My skills developed into a confident and competent nurse carrying a patient load of twelve patients; starting IVs, head to toe assessment, paper charting, entering orders in the computer, assisting doctors, preparing patients for surgery and procedures. My struggles and challenges in the workplace continued with women who hated me and wanted to see me fired. I wrestled with wanting to be accepted and liked by my peers who often tried to walk all over me and take advantage of me, but my strong side refuse to settle. I am a fighter.

~Divine Inspiration: Your faith can move mountains. The encounter of impossible obstacles are allowed to motivate and increase our strength God has placed inside of us.~

CHAPTER 17

Bernard & Monterio

MY WAY OF controlling and restraining Bernard when I worked the night shift was locking the wrought iron door and hiding the key within the house.Since we only lived five to eight minutes away from the hospital if there were an emergency I could easily tell them where the key was hidden. When it came to raising boys I was naïve and often wondered if Bernard's rebellious behavior was due to his father not being a part of his life. He was big for his age and could easily pass for sixteen. Every week he was suspended from school for bullying other boys, fighting, disrespecting the teachers' classroom and I was constantly reenrolling him back in school every week. He was suspended so many times I lost count. Even though his behavior was rebellious and defiant I realized he had a gift of art and drawing after winning the National Elementary Drawing Contest in the sixth grade. His teacher called recommending I enroll him in Overton High School, an optional school for exceptionally talented and gifted children. I thought this would be a wonderful opportunity if his behavior would get better.

~Divine Inspiration: Quiet, be still! God gives us quietness in the midst of our raging storms releasing our inner strength and comfort Mark 4:39~

When the school term ended the summer months were worse. One day I received a call from the security guard at Kroger Grocery store asking me to come pick up my son. I immediately drove up to Kroger, not knowing what to expect. Arriving at the store Bernard and a friend were being held in the security office for stealing plums and peaches hidden in their underwear. Another time I was called by the security guard at Sears department store where he was being detained for stealing name brand socks. Another incidence there was a loud knocking at my front door. Rushing to the door Bernard stood with a scared look on his face. I quickly opened the door and he came running past me to his room. A car pulled up into my driveway hurriedly with a man jumping out yelling, "Your son stole my son's bike out our front yard." He angrily proceeded to pick up his son's bike that Bernard evidently had just gotten off to run in the house, placing it in the trunk of his car. I apologized to the man repeatedly as he drove out the driveway. I didn't understand his interest in little six year old boy bikes. He continued stealing bikes as if he was obsessed. If no one was on the bike he stole it.

One Saturday morning I noticed all the screws were crooked in the front storm door and the glass was loose. I became suspicious when I saw Bernard was still sleeping which was unusual for him on a Saturday morning. He was always up bright and early eating a bowl of cereal and playing his video game or watching cartoon. While examining the door Monterio walked up to me and said, "Momma Bernard know how to get out the house at night." I asked him, "How?" He immediately began spilling his guts, "Last night while you was at work Bernard unscrewed the window out the storm door and took my bike and put it through the window. He told me to lock the wood door and go back to bed. Then he came back about 6:30 in the morning and I unlocked the door." I realized why he was still sleeping and had the nerves to be snoring on top of that. After getting the full story from his brother I woke Bernard not mentioning his brother spilling it on him. When asked about the storm door screws being loose he denied he knew anything about it, but a mother knows when her child is lying. That night getting ready for work setting the alarm noticed the alarm was changed to 4:00 a.m. I never set my clock for 4:00a.m. I knew Bernard had to be the one to alter the clock. Remembering he was talking to a girl name LaQuinta I went in his room and demanded her phone number. I called her home and spoke to LaQuinta's mother feeling a responsibility to inform her mother what our children had plotted together while we were at work. Talking to her she seem very resistant to hearing the truth stopping me abruptly asking, "Do ya'll live in those apartments?" Pausing in my tracks I realized this woman was trying to judge me. I proceeded to tell her we lived in a house. Extremely proud to have my own home I placed emphasis on the word house. Determined to make her listen to what our teenagers had plotted together I proceeded to tell her about discovering the storm door tampered with, the alarm clock being reset and how his baby brother told on him. She finally let her guards down and we talked for over two hours ending with her thanking me. She said she was going to remove LaQuinta's phone out of her room and Bernard was not allowed to see her anymore.

~Divine Inspiration: Love assumes the best in others.
If someone inadvertently causes you hurt and pain, you
choose to forgive and think only of the good that resides
in that person.~

Bernard began dating much older girls and hanging out with older guys and the wild and rebellious lifestyle elevated to another level. One night while working the 11-7 shift I received a call from the police Bernard and two other boys were being arrested for breaking and entering a vending machine at a car wash. I rushed home finding him sitting in the back seat of the police car. His juvenile record had plummeted and the judge decided on a stiffer penalty placing him in Tall Trees, an adolescent home for teenage boys, who needed aggressive discipline and training in society. I worried because this was his first incarceration but deep down I knew with him being big for his age he could take care of himself being known as somewhat of a bully. He was so muscular at a young age that people asked me if he worked out.

Bernard wasn't always a bully reflecting back while living on Wabash in our small one bedroom duplex, a boy a year older than Bernard and slightly taller lived next door bullied him every time he went outside to play running Bernard in the house afraid. I pulled him to the side looked him straight in his eyes and said, "That boy is the same age as you, and if you continue to let him bully you he will. I want you to fight back when he hit you again because that is the only way he will leave you alone." I said those words with intense sincerity straight from my heart to his heart. It hurt me to see my son bullied and intimidated to the point it kept him afraid to go outside. The very next day, looking out the window unknowingly to Bernard I watched him chase that boy across the yard, then dived on his back bringing him to the ground, beating him with both fists, running the boy in the house crying. I couldn't help but smile to myself. Sometimes all our children need is a word of encouragement to build confidence and boldness in their life.

After spending several months in Tall Trees Bernard was released on probation and enrolled back in Hillcrest High, but in less than one month he was suspended and transferred to Hamilton High School. In only a few weeks he was suspended again for fighting and loitering in the halls. Violating his probation he was sent back to Juvenile Court and placed on house arrest. When he violated this regulation he was sent to Somerville, Tennessee approximate 500 miles from home in to a Juvenile Correctional Facility where he stayed for eight months. With good behavior and communicating with his counselor Bernard was able to manipulate the judicial system so well he was sent back to Memphis to Memphis Recovery Center located on Poplar Ave in an old historic home in Midtown for drug assistance for young boys. I was thankful for programs like this to assist and discipline problem teenage boys with rebellious attitudes. Bernard was enrolled in Central High an optional school. I was hoping for a better education and changes in his behavior. A mothers' hope is never dead. Bernard's troubled and rebellious lifestyle continued throughout his teenage years, at seventeen he began selling drugs making it his own occupation. The tough dangerous street life did not end. He no longer attended school but took pride in rising early every morning, ironing and starching his clothes as if he was going to somebody job to stand on a corner to sell drugs. Talking to him didn't do any good and it was too much for me to handle.

~Divine Inspiration: Hold thoughts of love and see love in our children, this can lead to a fulfilling life, realizing trouble comes to pass not to stay.~

At seventeen Bernard was arrested for selling crack cocaine. The judge shook his head locking him up at to 201 Poplar adult jail with a court date. Refusing a public defender he called from jail to tell me he wanted a real attorney to defend him and told me where to find money he had hidden in the house. I found $20,000 in the back of his childhood television he received for Christmas when he was nine years old. I took the money to an attorney and he was released out on bond that same day with a court date and probation. This became a revolving door with the attorneys, locked up in jail, bond setting, selling drugs, buying cars, expensive clothes, and shoes. He was living the fast street life at full force and it was tearing me apart. Nothing I said changed his fast lifestyle. He was headstrong, stubborn, wild, addicted to living the fast lifestyle; selling drugs, fast money, buying cars, and shooting guns at his enemies throughout the neighborhood.

Then one night I received a phone call in the middle of the night that he was in a terrible accident. When I arrived on the scene there he was strapped on a stretcher being put in an ambulance. I jumped out my car and ran up to where he was and threw my arms around him crying. The paramedics pulled me away from him and rushed him to the hospital. Arriving to the hospital in the Emergency Room his blood pressure faded down to 60/40's. I watched the medical team hurriedly rushed to get his blood pressure up applying all kinds of monitors and IVs. I was afraid I was losing him and reached over to hug him crying out, "Oh Lord don't let my baby die." All of a sudden his blood pressure started to rise back to normal but he remain semiconscious. He told me later he experienced death and he felt his spirit leave his body going up to heaven and return back to his body. I believe God heard my cry and decided not to take him away from me yet. Bernard's fast life did not cease, he thought he was invincible.

One night while watching TV in the den, Terry and I heard gunshots hitting the side of the house. We jumped down to the floor scared for our lives until it was all over. I called Bernard and he rushed home finding his suburban truck filled with bullet holes parked on the side of the carport. A bullet also glazed the top of the carport attached to the house. It was obvious that Bernard had enemies and wanted to destroy him. I watched the rage fill his face looking at his badly damaged truck without saying a word jumped in his black Camaro and sped off. The next time I saw that Suburban it was painted a shiny candy apple red with brand new gold rims that turned heads when he drove down the streets. Only a few days after he was ambushed and shot by gang members while driving out some apartments. Bullets hitting him in his right side causing severe damage and internal bleeding to his right eye. He was taken to the Medical Regional Hospital emergency surgery and his right eye so badly damaged had to be removed. It was inevitable that something like this would eventually happen with the lifestyle he was living. This is a mothers' worse nightmare lying in bed at night wondering if he was safe, praying to hear his voice the next day. Meanwhile I knew his eye was lost forever and the unbearable pain penetrated the core of my soul, crying myself to sleep asking God, "Why?" But I knew why. It hurt me as bad as it hurt him. God allows everything to happen for a reason. After he was discharged from the hospital he went home with his girlfriend Jeanette. With so many burdens on me I was thankful she was there for him during this horrific crisis, even though the relationship didn't last long after that and he had to come back home.

~Divine Inspiration: Learning to wait on God to answer takes patience. We must learn how to wait with joy accompanied by the belief that what we need will be provided by God.~

After healing and adapting to having only one eye he still tried to go back to the streets to sell drugs again which was all he knew. Due to his handicap retiring from the streets sent him into a deep depression and pinned up anger he projected out toward me and everybody who came across his path. I couldn't take the hostility and resentment he carried toward the world and told him he had to go live with his grandmother. He slowly slipped deeper and deeper into depression, never leaving the house for anything. His livelihood of selling drugs was no longer a source of income. He felt he had nothing. No life. No money. No will to live. He had become a victim of his own inability.

Being a mother unable to watch him in so much pain notified Social Security Department to inquire and apply for his disability. He was denied but I encouraged him to write a letter pleading his case. His letter was so convincing and impressive and in approximate two weeks he began receiving benefits along with back pay. After he began receiving his checks and insurance benefits I contacted an ophthalmologist a specialist in making prosthetic eyes. I was amazed at how real the prosthetic eye looked with even tiny little blood vessels visible in the sclera. The prosthetic eye changed his appearance tremendously improving his attitude and confidence and he began leaving the house hanging out with some of his old friends. I was so happy to see him begin coming out of his shell but became suspicious at the same time. I asked questions but he said he just wanted to see his old friends.

He start spending most of his time with his best friend Mike the top dog drug dealer on the streets and the inevitable happened. He called ashamed and embarrassed confessing he was addicted to cocaine and needed help. I did what any mother would do. I started calling every rehabilitation center in Memphis until he was accepted. Although disappointed and hurt I did all I could to remain strong and control my emotions reflecting back to the members of my family who drugs had taken down and destroyed their lives. I had watched my sister walk the streets selling her body for drugs, selling everything she owned to buy crack cocaine, stealing money continuously from my mother to buy drugs until her early death at the age of 42. I remember the horrible stabbing death of my Uncle Theotria at 47 by his girlfriend that left him bleeding to death on the kitchen floor for a $20.00 to buy crack cocaine. Uncle Charles my mothers' youngest brother who drank excessively suffering with hypertension, gout, alcoholism and drug abuse dying at an early age of 43. With this running through my mind I wanted to find help for my son and save him from that powerful and deadly addicting white powder cocaine. He was admitted to Saint Francis Rehabilitation Program diagnosed with depression related to drug addiction from the psychological trauma of being shot and losing something as precious as an eye.

~Divine Inspiration: In the center of all our problems God is the solution. He is comfort, guidance, relief and healing. At the brink of a disaster He is salvation. God is the answer!~

MONTERIO

Monterio was a mommas' boy and there wasn't any doubt who was his father. The older he became the more he was the spitting image of Larry; the physique, hair, nose, skin complexion, and eyes. Refusing to accept any more abuse, disrespect and hostility in our marriage chose to separate myself and there was never a father-son relationship developed. Although during my pregnancy there was never any physical abuse there was the verbal and emotional abuse which continued. Our relationship was in the latter stages of ending, although afraid to be alone I stayed in a dysfunctional relationship much longer than I should have. After Monterio was born the physical abuse started back with intense arguments and fighting. I couldn't bear the abuse any longer although I wanted my son to have a father son relationship.

Monterio was the youngest so I tried to shield him. We had a very close relationship. I can remember when he would sing beautiful love ballads around the house and I knew he had a gifted voice. I would ask him to sing to me. Those were some the most treasured moments to have my song singing to me. Growing up Monterio was quiet and kept to himself and loved to watch television. I didn't have any problems with him in school, he was a good student. Being the brother of Bernard I didn't have to worry about him being bullied on at school. Bernard was well known throughout the Whitehaven area. During his sophomore and junior years he was more active and start working on his first part-time job at fifteen at Marlowes' a well-known restaurant in Whitehaven near Elvis Presley's home. He started as a dishwasher then he was promoted to a cook. Working diligently every day after school for four to five hours he saved enough money to purchase a little blue Chevrolet Neon blue car. He called it *Blue Bird.* I think this was the epitome of his junior high year. Choosing a good, economical, and reliable vehicle was a challenge. My daddy always told me to make sure you look at the mileage so I pass this on to Monterio in what to look for when buying a car. Another very important aspect to consider is to make sure he was insured which would mean my insurance rates would go up. Although he was a fulltime student on Honor Roll he was eligible for a good student discount that helped out a lot. Any parent who does not insure their teenager is showing a lack of judgment. Teens fear less because of less experience and have not witnessed many collisions, therefore they are prone to taking greater risks based on less good judgment.

~Divine Inspiration: Sons are a heritage from the Lord, children a reward from him. Like arrows in the hands of a warrior are children born in one's youth. Psalm 127:3-4~

Driving home from school one day Monterio was hit a teenage boy that was crossing the street causing him a fracture of the femur bone in his leg. The child wasn't seriously injured and the security of being insured was so rewarding. The insurance representative took care of everything, contacting the child's parents and arranging to pay all the medical bills. During his senior year he asked a young girl name Summer to the prom and being a proud mother I rented him a brand new Chrysler. He was always responsible and didn't cause me any problems so I didn't mind giving him the best to make him happy. After graduation in 2000 we moved into a beautiful newly built home in a very nice subdivision. I was blessed with a lovely brick home with three bedrooms with an expanded room upstairs. I even had a garage and a fireplace for the first time in my life. I truly loved our new home and bought all new furniture and decorated it just the way I liked. Monterio seemed to really love our new home and continued to work at Marlowe's until after graduation then his teacher helped him get a job at the International Airport. Then the day came when he moved into his first apartment. Being a mother who didn't want to let go of the strings tried every trick in the book to make him change his mind but deep inside I knew it was time for him to leave his mother's nest. Surprisingly he did remarkably well out on his own managing his bills and working everyday very responsibly as a mature young man making me so proud. I realized this was the best thing for him.

~Divine Inspiration: Love does not hurt. It is the experience to be who we are and love other people just the way they are too.~

CHAPTER **18**

The Forbidden!

THE STRESS AND high demands of being a professional nurse my faith was challenged to the utmost working with a group of women who were proverbial wolves in sheep's clothing. The constant attacks, lies, jealousy, backbiting and strife continued, but I trusted in God. They smile in my face then sabotage my work performance going to the nurse manager with allegations and write-ups. They were false friends and manipulators trying to lead me to think they were acting in my best interest when all the time they were stabbing me in the back to my boss. Little did I realize I am a child of God, a daughter of the King of Kings created a little lower than the angels with a unique and privileged purpose that belongs to no one else but me. I should never be manipulated into compromising my royal identity to con artists with poisonous apples up their sleeves. In fact little did I know there will be plenty of wolves in this world to harm me and I must learn to recognize them when they cross my path.

Being a single mother things in my life seem to get worser trying to juggle the night shift, troublesome women on my job, everyday life situations, and dealing with raising a rebellious son became overwhelming. Constantly taking inventory I realized I was surrounded by people who didn't have my best interest at heart. I decided if they weren't committed for my ultimate good I should dismiss them out of my life. Every trial increased my faith and drew me closer to forming a relationship with God. God allows trials in our lives to make us not break us and to bring us closer to him. If we find ourselves in a different trial, we will cause more harm if we try and run or rebel against it. Little did I realize developing faith is a process and the only way to fight the wiles of your enemies is to pray, read God's Word daily and pray fervently or you will fall short. God provides comfort and peace which gives us the strength to handle our trials only when we have a full time relationship with Him.

~Divine Inspiration: Testing by God reveals what is inside our hearts and produces tremendous faith, strength and perseverance.~

The stress and problems became overbearing and not rooted in faith found no relief in any area of my life. One night while working a 3-11 shift I was pulled to an oncology unit and one of my patients called out for a pain pill. It was an extremely busy shift and after finally arriving to her room with the pill found the patient had fallen asleep. Instead of properly disposing of the drug I innocently dropped the drug in my lab coat pocket thinking I would waste with another nurse when caught up with my work. Hours later I reached into my pocket for a pen when I realized the pill was still there. Tired and exhausted from working a very busy shift I did the forbidden and took the pill. In a matter of minutes a feeling of euphoria, pleasure and relaxation come over me making everything tolerable. The people I had worked with all evening were easier to deal with, my frustration and anger seem to go away. I seem to find what I wanted in this drug. On another occasion a patient requested a sleeping pill but when I entered the room found the patient asleep. I innocently put the pill in my pocket not remembering it until arriving home when clearing out my pockets. That night in bed tossing and turning unable to sleep decided to take the sleeping pill not recalling when I fell asleep. The next morning I was unable to lift my head off my pillow. It felt like my head weighed a 100 pounds. Lying in bed frightened but amazed at the effect of such a tiny pill, I began to talk to God promising Him I would never take another sleeping pill as long as I live and to this day I haven't.

~Divine Inspiration: A discouraged soul is in a helpless state, being neither able to "stand against the devil's schemes." Ephesians 6:11~

Nursing is a highly esteemed profession and because of the demanding and stressful nature of the job, along with nurses own personal issues in their lives, many nurses have fallen into the traps of substance abuse. "It has been estimated that 10 to 15 percent of all nurses in the U.S. are addicted to some type of illegal or controlled substance," explained a nurse anesthetist educator and member of the peer assistance program at the American Association of Nurse Anesthetists. The risk of addiction is not limited to any one specialty, the specialties with the highest prevalence of substance abuse uses are ICU, ER, OR and anesthesia. There are several reasons for nurses to fall into substance abuse: job stress, the work area, easy access to medications, family and children problems and workaholic personality. No matter how confident an impaired nurse may seem she/he can not provide safe, appropriate patient care when they are consumed with an addiction. Addiction is considered a disease and must be treated. With easy access to drugs I started stealing narcotics once a shift and increased more and more until I stole on the unit every chance I got. It didn't matter what floor of the hospital I worked I found a way to get drugs as my addiction escalated. Addiction is something that creeps into your life and once it happens you are trapped. Its defined as a chronic, relapsing brain disease that is characterized by compulsive drug seeking and use despite harmful consequences. Even though I was risking everything I had worked so hard to accomplish my brain had become diseased, practically stealing narcotics on a regular basis. My early stages of addiction started with using a pain pill a shift as a coping mechanism to distract attention from my problems, gaining a euphoric feeling engaging in enjoyable conversation, and restoring my energy.

~Divine Inspiration: Do not yield to discouragement no matter how severely stressed or consumed by our problems we may be.~

Chemical dependency is also defined as a state of psychological and or physical addiction to chemical substances. A substance disorder does not discriminate according to economic, class, age, ethnic background or gender. This disease is a progressive and chronic disorder and if left untreated can become fatal. I had definitely become addicted and the more I took the more I wanted and the worst my situation got. My whole career was being jeopardized but I was receiving everything I wanted from this drug. It made me feel good, it made me forget about my worries, it made me feel confident, increased my self-esteem, and even made the night hours pass faster working the night shift. I no longer dwelt on all my problems. The drugs had become my escape.

~Divine Inspiration: One of the greatest challenges of creating an abundant life is taking full accountability for what you do and how you do it.~

As my dependency and addiction progressed the satisfaction of using drugs diminished and more drugs were required for me to feel the same pleasure received in the beginning stages of my addiction. Having access to all the narcotics on the units I increased my usage going from the pills to vials of medication to stealing boxes of drugs to supply my addiction while away from the hospital. I asked myself, "Have you lost your mind." I was stoned addicted to narcotics. I was at the point of doing the unthinkable. I didn't expect God to listen to my prayers so I didn't bother to pray. Why should he listen? I hadn't been in nobody's church for years. I hadn't read my bible in years. My life was slipping away from me. At night before going to work I would tell myself, "I am not going to use drugs tonight. I can quit when I get ready. I still have control over this addiction. That was the farthest thing from the truth. The truth was I was totally addicted to narcotic drugs and I did not have any control over my flesh. Every night the drug cycle would start the beginning of the shift until the end. I was totally sick, helpless and needed help.

My work performance remained satisfactory, competent and skilled with excellence, at least that's what I told myself. Nursing school had prepared me well for the clinical environment with knowledge and nursing judgment to practice competent on a highly demanding unit. One night when I read the staff meeting written in the nurse communication folder by the nurse manager, it read, "If there is any nurse with a drug abuse problem please come to me so we can help." Denial is part of the disease and played a big role in my life. It was so obvious she was reaching out to me but my sick mind told me she wasn't talking to me and there must be someone else who has a drug problem. She could of easily ordered a random drug screen and I would have lost my license forever.

~Divine Inspiration: Have mercy on me, O God, have mercy! I look to you for protection. I will hide beneath the shadow of your wings until this violent storm is past Psalm 46:1.~

So deep in denial I continued to feed my addiction which was totally out of control taking large volumes of narcotics on the unit and stealing boxes to take home on the weekend to feed my addiction. Getting down on my knees every night before going to work I would ask God to please deliver me from this addiction. I begged Him to remove the desire for drugs. But every night my flesh surrendered to my addiction starting the drug cycle all over again.

~Divine Inspiration: Whenever you face trials of many kinds regard it as joy, delight in it and God will reward your faith James 1:2

CHAPTER **19**

God Help!

AS MY ADDICTION continued to advanced to the destructive stage I was not only in denial but also regret. My disease had lasted long enough and penetrated deeply enough in my life and mind that cause me to feel a sense of regret. The destructive nature of the disease was forming a empty space in my soul. The addiction had expanded similar to a malignant cancerous tumor that progressively invaded my life, attitude, personality and mind. I had began to deny what the truth was to others and to myself in all matters in the defense of my addiction. I started out with my drug of choice being Demerol but now it didn't matter I was taking everything I could get my hands on. The drugs had become so important I was willing to sacrifice my soul. Amazingly we are all given an ample about of time on earth to fulfill our ordain destiny given to us by God. It is our responsibility to choose to walk with God in order to follow that destiny. But some way or another we fall short and end up in our valleys and pitfalls of life. We all make mistakes that we regret and the guilt hold us in shackles, torturing us with the images of what we should of done or accomplished had we not made the wrong decisions.

Even though we make the wrong choices and decisions in life we must remember that God is always ready with open arms to forgive us. He is so merciful all the time and will forgive us for our sins. We must lift ourselves up to repentance and let the claws of sin fall down from all around, correct the sinfulness, and take responsibility for our sins and move beyond the guilt. We all want success but success is not measured in the accomplishing of material possessions and wealth. We are wealthy only because God loves us. Gods' grace and mercy is a beautiful gift he gives to all his children here on this earth. But somehow my relationship with God had diminished and I was walking in darkness feeling as if I was floating in a river trying to keep my ship anchored or tied to the dock in a spiritual fog. I desperately needed the peace of God to comfort my heart.

~Divine Inspiration: Remember we are never without God who is our pilot of the plane when we do not know which way to turn the wheel.~

Addiction is characterized by a compulsive drug use of any type and I was consumed in my addiction using more and more drugs without any restraints. While each drug produced a different physical effect, they all shared one thing in common, producing a feeling of euphoria effecting largely on the motivation and pleasure pathways of the brain causing my brain to remember to always want more. Working the night shift I continued to use drugs despite the negative consequences. My need for drugs grew to be more important than anything else including; family, friends, career, and even my own health. My need to use drugs was so strong that my mind found ways to deny or rationalize the addiction convincing myself I needed drugs to cope with my problems at home, to deal with the vindictive women I worked with every night. I even told myself I could stop whenever I wanted to.

Drugs made me feel good or stopped me from feeling bad. I realized I had become a true addict when I found myself increasingly relying on using drugs every single night I came to work. For my off days I stole boxes of Demerol, Dilaudid or Morphine along with insulin syringes to draw up the drug and inject myself in the subcutaneous tissues. I was gone mad. I had lost total control and my thinking was off. "God Please Help me," I cried. With my nursing career being in danger I continued to use drugs on the unit every chance I got. I wanted to quit so badly. But every time I tried I would experience extreme irritability, frustration, rudeness, restlessness, depression, anxiety, nervousness, a bad attitude which was severe withdrawals. My flesh always surrendering to the addiction telling myself, "I will only use just this once, just so I can get over this edge. But it didn't stop there and I became once again powerless to drugs.

. *~Divine Inspiration: Dear Restless Heart, peace comes from God only, His love comforts and corrects every wrong and sorrow in your life.~*

CHAPTER 20

Far and Beyond

I MET JOHNATHAN an electrician at Baptist Hospital who made a pass at me and offered to fix any home electrical repairs in my home giving me his phone number. I thought he was kind of cute and I was impressed with his electrical skills. I gave him a call and he fixed everything I needed fixing in my house. We began a relationship and one night while at his house he pulled out some crack cocaine and start smoking. Stupefied at what I saw I was speechless. Then he offered the drug to me but I quickly refused. Crack cocaine the most potent form of cocaine is 75%--100% pure, far stronger than regular cocaine. Considered a drug sold on the streets known as rock, work, hard, iron, and crack the most addictive form of cocaine. I was afraid of crack cocaine and more disappointed in Johnathan a man whom I was impressed with, was really a crack addict.

Being afraid of cocaine didn't last long, we smoked crack cocaine every weekend with him spending his entire paycheck and borrowing money from me. We drove through some of roughest area of town looking for crack until wee hours of the morning. The more we smoked the more we wanted. An addict doesn't quit until they either run out of money or all the drug dealers have retired for the night. When there was no more crack to smoke we would go back to his place feeling low and discouraged. One night I watched him literally crawl on his hands and knees on the floor combing the carpet with his fingers hoping to find cocaine crumbs. After spending a weekend with Johnathan the next day I felt miserable. What was wrong with me? I was using narcotics on my unit at the hospital and smoking crack cocaine from the streets. I never felt so low in my life. I felt like scum. I was so ashamed. I felt so heavy and low-spirited sinking more and more into depression. My sons and family did not have any idea I was battling with a drug addiction. I was still functioning because I knew I would get more drugs when I went back to work.

~Divine Inspiration: God uses His refining fire to burn away our sins and impurities and then gloriously come to our rescue to bring us closer to Him.~

After having used drugs all night on the unit one morning my supervisor asked to come in her office. I had ignored her messages in the communication folder when she asked if a nurse had a chemical dependency problem to come forth for help. Entering her office I immediately noticed a very concerned look on her face. Taking a seat sitting across from her at her desk she looked me directly in the eyes with that concerned look and asked, "Do you have a drug problem Christine?" Looking in her eyes without looking away I answered, " No." She proceeded to tell me, " If I send you to the lab to have a blood test drawn and the results are positive for drugs you will be terminated from your job. If you admit you have a drug problem Methodist will provide you the help you need by allowing you to go through a Drug Rehabilitation Program and you will be able to keep your job." Embarrassed and full of shame I looked down and muttered, "Yes I do." It took every ounce of strength in my body to admit to her I had a drug problem. I had come to the Red Sea in my life. There was no way out, there was no way back. I had to go through. I had to dare to trust God. Dare to follow Him. From one black woman to another she understood all the sacrifices that comes with becoming a young black nurse in a career where few black women make it. She made a few calls making arrangements for me to enter into Rehabilitation Program. All I could think, "How am I going to do this? What will I do with Monterio?" I didn't have to be concerned about Bernard he was already locked up in a Correctional Center for adolescents.

~Divine Inspiration: When God has a purpose for your life, He will rise you up above all tribulations.~

My life had turned into a great big mess. I needed my job and loved being a nurse. I was willing to do whatever it took to keep my livelihood. Of course I had my share of trials but it did not outweigh the joy and satisfaction I received being a nurse. Although nursing was a calling God had placed on my life, I saw nursing as my security blanket, with its infinite knowledge, information, and opportunities.

After hanging up the phone she told me I needed to go home collect a few things and a bus from Methodist would pick me up to check me in the Methodist OutReach Drug Rehabilitation Center that same day. I arranged for my father to pick up Monterio from school and take him to my mothers' house then packed a few things to take with me. I sat on the living room sofa to wait on the bus while gazing out the storm door uneasy and embarrassed. My life seemed like a high mountain that was growing higher and higher while I hung on with dear life. When the fear began engulfing me I reminded myself of what God had already done for me. This always seem to increase my faith reflecting back to nursing school, buying my first home, raising two sons as a single mother and surviving an abusive marriage. Would he leave me now? His word says, " I will never leave you or forsake you." But I knew His word belong to His children who loved and obeyed Him.

Overcoming trials and tribulations make faith strong but sometimes our faith weakens and we forget. I knew I could trust God and he will take me farther than this irrational fear, but this spirit of addiction had it claws deep in my soul. Fear paralyzed me. I wondered what kind of place am I about to enter into. What kind of people am I going to be around? I wished there was some way out, but there wasn't. I still thought to myself, if I had prayed harder or tried harder I could have avoided all this embarrassment in my life. What will people think and say? I was taking a step from the known to the unknown. At some point in life we all will be faced with the known to the unknown.

The question is was I ready to move from the sinful drug seeking lifestyle to obedience to Gods' will for my life? The truth of the matter is, I didn't know what I was ready for. I was lost without a relationship with God. I desperately needed the power of Jesus Christ to take the next step moving me from the sinful life to salvation. In reality an addict can only receive help when totally honest with himself. If never confronted by my supervisor in her office giving me an ultimatum to keep my job or face termination I would still be using drugs. But God's sweet grace placed me under pressure by an understanding supervisor who cared enough to take the time to counsel me. The disease is sickening and it made me sick. I thought I could control it but it had controlled me for five years. Being possessed by this demon I couldn't shake it alone. I needed help!

~Divine Inspiration: Because we are favored and loved when we don't deserve it, grace encourages us to dust off and keep going when we fall or when life gets hard Philippians 3:14~

CHAPTER **21**

"Restoration"

ARRIVING TO THE Methodist Outreach Rehabilitation Center for a 28 day residential treatment program a sense of peace came over me. I had fought this terrible addiction for five long years which had taken over my life. I was so tired. My prayers were answered not in the way I had asked but with God right in the center of my blessings. It was a blessing to have an opportunity and a second chance to get my life together and start over. I was ready to surrender by taking the first step in the program, admitting I had a drug addiction and I had loss all control of my life and accepting the fact I needed a Higher Power someone other than myself. The first thing the program is designed to teach are methods of interacting in a drug free environment and not associating with friends who still used drugs. The 12 step program encouraged addicts not only to stop using alcohol and drugs, but to examine and change habits related to the addiction. Research has proved that effective treatment addresses the multiple needs of the patient rather than treating addiction only, because in every addicts' life there is a root issue involved that cause them to choose a life of using drugs or alcohol. Statistics show there are millions of people willingly admitting they need to be admitted into a drug rehabilitation program. The age group with the most admissions to a drug rehabilitation center is 25-29, 59.9% were Caucasian, 20.9% were African Americans, 13.7% were Hispanics. Researchers say nurses are more likely to face substance abuse disorders than the general population. Because of the long hours, constant stress and other pressures, as many as one in five Registered Nurses may face addiction issues during their careers, according to the American Nurses Association. Every year, hundreds of nurses in the US have their license impended or revoked because they harmed a patient, diverted or misappropriated drugs, and couldn't safely practice because of their addiction.

~Divine Inspiration: You can not make a wounded person go beyond where they are willing to go. We must honor their boundaries. Honor their choices and when they are ready to be healed they will be.~

My first days were filled with despair and discouragement trying to adjust to the new environment. I sat alone in my room reflecting back over my life thinking how did my life end up here. The program required my full participation in the meetings in order for insurance to pay. I'm certain there were ways to verify my progress and participation. In my first group session I met so many broken souls from all walks of life with one major thing in common, an addiction too big to handle. They reached out to share hope to the newcomers starting their journey to recovery. Sharing my experiences of a life living on drugs became comfortable in a group of people who were like me. I found that drug addiction is universal and I was not alone. Day three I met Eric Davidson, who was admitted for cocaine abuse and his job had presented him with the same ultimatum as me. We became more than friends, almost inseparable at times, holding hands, walking and sitting together at all the meetings. Instead of focusing on the program we were focusing 100% on each other. A counselor at the facility approached us in the halls and warned us we were together too often and our behavior was inappropriate. We began writing each other long love letters and fed off each other's attention. I thought he was my soul mate, the love I had been waiting for all my life.

~Divine Inspiration: Sorrow and despair that is endured in the right spirit impacts our growth and bring us to a higher sense of love and compassion for others.~

After weeks of meetings and group sessions sharing about the journey of a drug abused life and hearing others share their stories we developed a bond gaining a sense of belonging and acceptance. The environment was safe to practice our new behavior without the fear of failure or rejection learning the most important thing to realize is we all are responsible for our own life, our own actions, and our own choicest. Spending time with Eric helped lift me out of the pit of depression adding a spark to my life which carried me forward to persevere and complete the twenty eight days. He was discharged from the program in two weeks, an insurance issue but came back every evening to the outpatient group sessions. I really cared about him and I felt he cared about me, unfortunately we met at an awkward time in our lives when we were both sick with a disease and the only person who could heal us was a Higher Power. We were introduced to Him in the program but did not develop a committed relationship, instead we focused on each other. We were not strong enough in our recovering process and the relationship ended.

The experience of a inpatient rehabilitation program and becoming friends with a group of people that had one thing in common, a disease caused by drugs, will always hold a special place in my heart that changed my life in such a profound way. We all shared some of the most heartbreaking stories and even cried together about some of the most horrific times in our lives. On the day of my discharge you would think I would be happy to be leaving but actually I was not. I had grown comfortable and safe here. There were no drugs to temptation, the people all understood me, there were no worries. It was like my Safe Haven and I liked it here. I wanted to stay just one more week. It was time to go, this season was over.

~Divine Inspiration: God's everlasting love always reveal your loss, but then you will see how He used it to break the evil chains that had you bound.~

CHAPTER **22**

A Lifetime Journey

THE TWENTY EIGHT days of inpatient called for a time of intense work and profound learning of skills in my long-term struggle for sobriety, but now it was time to apply those skills in the real world. The process continued with attending five weeks of outpatient therapy and nurse conduit therapy group meeting three times a week. Eric continued attending the evening outpatient meetings but I focused on the program reading my recovery books diligently beginning to rise to a new level of faith trusting God in my recovery process. It is a process that doesn't just last for 28 days but a process that is a lifetime journey, almost impossible to do alone without the support and guidance of people to lean on for encouragement. I was learning to trust God more than ever for guidance on my journey as a recovering nurse on my road to freedom.

Research has revealed that the long term recovery outlook for anyone who struggles with substances abuse is glum, that only 10% will succeed in recovery. These are horrible statistics but its the truth. Entering back into the real world felt strange and awkward experiencing irrational fear that almost paralyzed me from going forward. Reflecting on God's promises gave me enough faith to face my fears. Having experienced something that had changed my life, I was no longer the same person twenty-eight days ago consumed with a disease of addiction which took over my whole entire life.

Returning back to the unit there were certain restrictions; no administrations of narcotics, random drug screening for two years, mandatory aftercare meetings for six weeks, mandatory conducive meetings for nurses only for six weeks, and working 40 hours a week left me exhausted and drained at the end of the week. I thought once I was sober God would lay a yellow brick road before me and I would go skip pity- do all day. However in reality Rehab was just the beginning of an on-going, life-long journey with the hardest work beginning ahead of me after leaving the Rehab facility. Rehab provided safety and security and a world free of temptation where there was a support network leading us in the direction to a life free of drugs and alcohol. Unfortunately for an addict in the real world there comes everyday stress which can easily trigger the temptation to turn back to drugs daily. Difficult times and places are our schools of faith and character.

~Divine Inspiration: Paul the apostle said, "We are hard pressed on every side, but not crushed; perplexed, but not in despair; persecuted, but not abandoned; struck down, but not destroyed Corinthians 4:8~

Filled with a whole lot of guilt and shame it was extremely difficult for me to face the people on my unit. The stares, gossip, pointing of finger, ridicule with some even refusing to talk to me. I felt so alone, humiliated and annihilated just as I had anticipated. I continued to trust in my Higher Power to help me get through one day, one hour, one minute at a time. They teach you in Rehab that you only have one day at a time nothing more or nothing less. My self-esteem seemed to crumble, no longer shielded by my friends in Rehab, but met with ridicule and strife every way I turned. I read my Daily Devotional Recovery Book religiously every opportunity sometimes isolating myself in the ladies room to meditate and read to gain strength, hope, and consolation. This was definitely a valley experience and no one, not my mother, my father, my brother, my sons could help me go through it. No one but the mighty hand of God.

Nurse Carolyn RN the charge nurse made my life a living hell working under her humiliating me every opportunity she got. With certain restrictions, I was not allowed to administer narcotics for six months and whenever my patients needed a narcotic I had to ask nurse Carolyn to administer it. In exchange she would assign me two or three of her patients each night whether any of my patients needed pain medicine or not. This was humiliating and I didn't think I could endure the shame.

~Divine Inspiration: Do not allow deceptive intelligence to make you believe there are no lessons to be learned exactly where you are, doing exactly what you are doing today. "There we saw the Giants" Numbers 13:33

Giants represent the great difficulties that stalk us in our lives, in our families, our churches, our social life, workplace and even in our own hearts. There were times when despair and hopelessness seem to engulf me. I had come to far to quit. I must overcome the giants or they would devour me.

My recovery books were my safety net, my consoler and

the more I read them the closer my relationship with God developed and my faith begin to flourish giving me the strength to handle the challenges and attacks from my enemy. With enemies on my left and on my right, nurses writing me up every week the pressure and stress of dealing with attitudes, haters became overwhelming. One morning my manager called me in her office to discuss another write up from a nurse. She began to expound on the allegations by a nurse, when I interrupted her saying "Look I can't help these nurses don't like me. I can not believe you call me in here about every little thing they write me up about." From that day forward she never called me in her office again. The hateful remarks and attitudes from the nurses continued and I began to fester bitterness in my soul. Bitterness has a tenacious way of taking root deep within the soul and resist all efforts to weed it out. As time went on the pain and hurt only seem to sharpen. I knew that a bitter heart destroys your spirit and take away your joy but with God's grace He is able to reach down and remove bitterness and bring total healing. Refusing to allow bitterness to take root in my life with God's help learn to replace bitterness with forgiveness.

~Divine Inspiration: "Make sure no root of bitterness spring up, causing trouble and by it defiling many." Hebrews 12:15~

Continuing to grow in my spiritual faith reading my AA books learning to cope with every day stressors, persecution, rejection and pain I learned to obey my Higher Power. I learned to shut my ears to the negative forces all around me and listen to His spirit speak to me with an inexpressible tenderness, power and comfort. My spirit drank the words of my daily devotions and it enabled me to face life's adversities, like a withered flower that absorbed the rain from the sky restoring it petals to spring forth again. Although a stronger and wiser nurse but my fellow peers would not accept me for who I had become. Tired of working alongside people who only saw who I use to be, instead of who I had become, a new and transformed nurse who wanted to advance to higher heights. A nurse who wanted to pursue her career and follow her dream of becoming a registered nurse one day. A nurse who wanted to be accepted by her peers as someone who is honest, trustworthy, and a diligent professional healthcare worker. After my Rehab Program outpatient sessions and random drug screening was over I felt like a woman who had gone through a metamorphosis, a woman who found God as her friend, who desired something more, something better for her life. No longer desiring to remain in a place where I was unappreciated and devalued I began looking for a transfer position on a different floor believing if I am no longer growing it is time to go further.

~Divine Inspiration: When I was a child, I talked like a child. When I became a woman, I put childish ways behind. God gives me His wisdom so I can understand His ways.Corinthians 13:11~

Even though not a Christian I began to develop a strong connection to God. The bible says we are to be conformed in the image of Jesus Christ, by repenting of our sins and believing that Jesus died on the cross for our sins and resurrected on the third day. Believing this in my heart and confessing this with my mouth I am saved. Even though I was a good person I am still a sinner and needed saving from my sins. Salvation is given to us by grace, through faith. There is nothing we did or ever can do, to deserve it. It's a free gift from God. All we have to do is receive it.

~Divine Inspiration: For it is with your heart that you believe and are justified, and it is with your mouth that you confess and are saved Romans 10:10~

CHAPTER **23**

Pursuit of Happiness

TRANSFERRING TO METHODIST Hospital downtown on 8b Tower to work rotating shifts I was hoping for an opportunity to work with people who didn't know about my past. Despite all the pain and humiliation in LPN school I never dreamed of wanting to return back to nursing school but there was a fire down in my soul that desired to go higher, to become better, to be more, and refuse to remain stagnant in the same area of my life. Significantly proud of my accomplishment as a LPN I knew in order to reach my professional goals and broaden my horizons, to broaden my intellectual curiosity, and increase my knowledge and skills I had to pursue a RN degree. Always suffering from low self esteem and a not good enough addiction I didn't have enough faith to dream or believe I could become an RN, therefore choosing to be a LPN. When you are a single mother living on welfare LPN seem more reachable, the program was shorter, required less general education and cost less.

With faith and trust in God I realized He allowed the storms in my life to make me stronger and draw me closer to Him, teaching me the path of faith, sorrow, suffering, tears, trials, conflicts, hardships, dangers, beatings, persecutions, misunderstanding, trouble, and distress, all is a part of carrying the Cross for Jesus. But the path of faith is also one of joy, healing comfort, smiles, victories, triumphs. God was there to meet me in the center of every trial turning them into blessings. In the bible Abraham thought himself as a father, even though he was 100 years old and his wife Sarah 98, because God said so. That is genuine faith-believing and declaring what God said, stepping out on what appears to be thin air and finding solid rock beneath the feet. My faith first began to flourish and develop in LPN school when God allowed everything I suffered to happen, pruning and preparing me for what lies ahead in my future. I seriously began to pursue advancing my career to become a Registered Nurse.

~Divine Inspiration: In all these things we are more than conquerors through him who loved us Romans 8:37. God calls things that are not as though they were Romans 4:17~

After being a LPN for five years, clean and sober for nearly three years, I was prepared to advance my nursing career. I was ready for a change in my life. Never being one who was afraid of change but open and willing to enter change if it benefited my life positively. Over the years I've learned change is inevitable. Some people are afraid of change. Either you accept change willingly or you are changed by force. It is always better to change willingly, when you have a choice in the matter. The doors we open and close each day decide the lives we live. After thorough research I chose a correspondence program to pursue my career which allowed me freedom and flexibility allowing me to work around my job schedule while raising two sons.

The Distance Learning System developed a Learning Module program to assist adult students with the opportunity to test out of many prerequisite courses. The program's philosophy is "what you know is more important than where or how you learned it." You are allowed to use prior credits and knowledge to earn a college degree and obtain additional credit by not making residency at a college a requirement, working at your own pace. For each exam you were given a study guide to prepare you for the exam which cost $60.00 but today has increased to $325.00 for each exam. Upon completion of the nursing theory exams you are eligible to take the (FCCA) Focused Clinical Competencies Assessment where you must demonstrate competency related to:

Head to toe assessment
Managing multiple patients
Working with Interdisciplinary teams

You are allowed two hours to complete each of the FCCA each includes a 10 minute tutorial and a five minute survey. After completing each assessment you will be mailed your results, Pass or Fail within 45 days from the testing date. I shared the information with my girlfriend Denise and we began the course together. She completed her course theory must faster then prepared to take the FCCA. Allowed only two errors during your clinical performance, it was so easy to be disqualified, this was the most challenging part of the program.

~Divine Inspiration: A vision will pull you forward.
A vision will motivate you. It will wake you up in the
morning. Your eyes will see more in your future.~

We heard that a co-worker failed the FCCA after taking a blood pressure was asked to repeat the blood pressure but failed to wait sixty seconds. The second error was a child patient he failed to wash his hands before leaving the room which disqualified him. Unfortunately while waiting to retake the exam experienced a heart attack leading to major heart surgery and he never completed the course. Denise prepared for the FCCA making all her travel arrangements, hotel fees but she was also disqualified for making similar errors. She was devastated saying it wasn't worth all the expenses when it was so easy to be disqualified. After hearing their experiences I decided to re-enroll at Shelby State Community College where I had college credit hours invested toward my nursing education.

Now with ten years gone by with procrastination a core hinder in my life finally enrolled. Procrastination is a form of slothfulness used as a coping mechanism, putting things off for another day, to keep stress under control, causing many missed opportunities. It is a spirit that has crippled my life and kept me from moving forward until one day I proclaimed, " I rebuke the spirit of procrastination." Then I made an oath to take any class or elective to stay enrolled until accepted in the LPN to RN Fast Track Associate Degree program. I was excited but fear kept rising its ugly head to deter me from chasing after my dream. I knew there were many challenges ahead and deep down I still had doubts of reaching my dream. I reminded myself to put my faith and trust in God and know He will not forsake me.

~Divine Inspiration: Can a woman forget her nursing child, or lack compassion for the child of her womb? Even if these forget, yet I will not forget you. Isaiah 49:15~

Therefore, through all my circumstances I had to hold on to the truth God sees me as His child just as a mother who has a keen sensitivity to her child. This is the most comforting promise God has given me to look forward to, that he will never forget me, and He is at my right hand.

~Divine Inspiration: I keep the Lord in my mind always. Because He is at my right hand, I will not be shaken Psalm 16:8~

CHAPTER **24**

A Dark Time

TRANSFERRING TO 8B Tower was an opportunity to start over in a new environment, hoping things would be better, but learned that faces change but people are the same everywhere; connivers, jealousy, backbiters, and negativity. It's always challenging starting over on a new unit, learning to cope with difficult people, something I've always struggled with; on my job, my family, school, and college. God made me realize that if my life was without struggles I would never be made stronger by looking up toward Him to lift me up. It is through the difficult times that God will lead us to greatness and our destiny and not through a life that's self-indulgent down a path of rose colored gardens. Transitioning from a night shift position to a day and evening rotation required significant adjustments in my daily routines and personal life. On the new unit with a nurse-patient ratio of 8:1 was more challenging than I ever imagined. Unfamiliar and inexperienced working on day and evening shift, things operated completely different from night shift with more duties and responsibilities: medications, procedures, surgeries, doctor rounding, orders, am care, meals, baths, linens change.

*~Divine Inspiration: When you feel the most forsaken
and alone, forge ahead knowing that God is near. He is in
the darkest cloud waiting for you.~*

One of the most important responsibilities of a nurse is
delegation. Delegation is one of the most difficult tasks that
licensed health care professionals face most of their careers.
It is entrusting the performance of a selected nursing task to
an individual who is qualified, competent, and able to perform such tasks. One of the reasons for delegation is it frees
nurses up to do what we've been trained and educated to do,
make clinical judgments about patients and coordinate patient care. There is a major problem in the healthcare system
where many nurses encounter tension and resistance when
delegating tasks to nursing assistants. This causes the nurse to
perform the task herself, most of the time just to get along, or
wanting to be liked, making the workload overbearing. There
has never been no doubt nurses need help on the unit and
have found myself encountering friction or confrontation with
a nursing assistants after delegating a task on multiple occasions throughout my career. This is a nation wide problem
with the root core being people do not like being told what
to do.

I continued pursuing my RN degree along with facing
challenge after challenge with my sobriety being tested daily. Slowly drifting away from my daily devotional reading I
began practicing some of my old behavior lifestyle habits.
Dealing with Bernard rebelliousness, an extreme demanding
and difficult job, working with difficult people, everything
seem to wrap its arms around me until I couldn't breathe anymore. I couldn't bear the struggle any longer. With no sobriety
friends to connect I reach for what I remembered to numb

my conscious mind, I reached for my consoler. My mind told me, "This is a new staff, they don't know anything about your history. Anyway you got this drug thing under control. You have been clean for almost three years. You can easily stop after this one time." Satan will always tell your mind what you want to hear

. ~*Divine Inspiration: Seek the spirit for motivation so the flesh will not be stimulated. God assures us that we will never face a shortfall of His grace to complete the purpose He has for our lives.*~

But I didn't stop! I kept using just as many narcotics as before admitted into Rehab or more. In addition to working through an agency going to other hospitals and nursing homes I got more drugs jeopardizing my whole career, my life, my sons lives. I became dangerously reckless signing out narcotics and it was no longer suspicious but obvious what was happening. Engulfed with guilt and shame I had reached the point of self destruction trapped by this disease once again. It had progressed beyond my control. Then one day the inevitable happened. I received a letter from The Board of Nursing Investigation Department. Not in the least surprised one of the hospitals through the agency had reported me. The hospital had brought allegations against me for stealing and abusing narcotics. They informed me I would be contacted by an agent from the Board of Nursing in a couple of days to handle my case. All I could think about is my license would be provoked and my career will be over.

Walking into to the Health Department downtown anxious and worried about my career looked intently for the agents' office. Entering the office I will never forget a tall black middle age gentlemen wearing a dark suit who politely greeted me as I took my seat. He proceeded to ask me about my career background and then presented me with the allegations brought against me. I had gone over in my head a thousand times what I would say in my defense which can be difficult to do when you know you are guilty. He listened intently while I pleaded my case displaying facial expressions that said he had heard hundreds of nurses pleading their case trying to save their license. I ended my testimony saying, " I am currently pursuing my RN degree." I noticed his eyebrows raised and he took his eyes off the paper he was making notes and asked me, "Where are you attending and how much longer do you have?" I knew this would make him look at me in a different perspective and I intentionally used this as part of my defense to help my case. Even though guilty of everything written in the letter, I believed he knew it too. By the Grace of God I was allowed a second chance giving me favor in the eyes of the agent. God is a God of second chances. Hallelujah! In a few weeks I received a letter from Tennessee Board of Nursing informing me the allegations filed against me was dropped after a thorough investigation. Oh what a heavy burden lifted. I was so thankful to God making a promise to never use narcotics again.

~Divine Inspiration: A guilty heart is destructive. It damages your self worth and erodes your self-respect.~

CHAPTER 25

Back On Track

SLIPPING THROUGH THE grips of the powerful and demonic stronghold that nearly destroyed my life a second time, I began to see nursing in a different light. It wasn't just a career, it was a calling. Caring for the sick and making a difference in their lives at a time when they feel helpless is rewarding and fulfilling no matter how small a deed, affecting lives from all walks of society. Even though fallen back into the grips of drugs caused my nursing career to be put on hold, I worked hard getting my life back on track, promising God to never use drugs no matter how difficult life gets. Major changes were happening on the floor, the nurse manager was leaving to pursue a corporate position leaving our unit without a manager which leads to disorganization and chaos. Most nursing staff feel helpless without someone to run to with their problems and complaints. Even though there was an interim manager it wasn't the same as having your own manager, the human face of the unit. There were rumors running rampant who was to get the position, shocking the whole hospital when nurse Terri Marr RN got the job. She was a rehire with 15 years experience working in the

Emergency Room.

Nurses who knew her when she formerly worked for the hospital had so many negative things to say, centered with bitterness and nasty remarks deliberately attempting to damage her reputation and undermine her credibility. Surprisingly meeting Terri Marr changed my entire life and had such a profound impact on my life to this very day. Never listen to what other people say about an individual, instead wait to get to know the person for yourself. And as I've found to be true many times their perception of her wasn't my perception at all. Terri Marr was the sweetest, kindest person I had ever met since becoming a nurse. I knew she was a Christian and loved the Lord by her behavior and the way she expressed kindness, gentleness with a soft tone in her voice when she spoke. Before being promoted to the nurse managers' role she was always found sitting alone at lunch or on break, never seen engaging in any form of malicious gossip or negative talk. Truly blessed to have known this guardian angel that God placed in my life for only a season, during one of the most difficult times of my life, RN school. I know Sovereign God played apart in the hiring of Terri Marr. She protected me from the enemy when I was being attacked and always supported me with my work schedule around my school schedule. I will never forget her and I will always love her dearly. Nursing school was made easier having a manager in my corner especially during the rough times when I thought I would be terminated from the program. Still carrying a not good enough addiction reflecting back to LPN school when the instructor scolded me saying, "You need to go into another field beside nursing" and placing me on probation. This negative stigma still remained and dwelt in my soul.

~Divine Inspiration: If God's desire is to increase your capacity, do not be frightened by the greater realm of the difficulties and challenges that lie ahead.~

A medical surgical nurse my whole nursing career, the obstetrics rotation was the most challenging class in RN school. I didn't know hardly anything about obstetric nursing. The class curriculum focused on writing care plans, lectures and four exams that were complex with questions consisting of two and three paragraphs with multiple choice answers. To thoroughly understand the question I had to read the question over and over worrying about running out of time. My score on the first exam only 62%. Extremely stressed and working very hard to bring my score to a passing grade made only 76 on the second exam, 82 on the third, leaving me needing to make 76 or more on the final exam in order to pass the course. My final grade was 76.4 only by the grace of God.

Graduating with an Associate Degree on April 24, 1994 I began preparing for state board examination, thinking I never thought I would ever be going through this torture again, but here I am. Never say what you will not do. Life has a way of making you swallow your own words. But this time I had more faith, knowledge and wisdom and understood what it took to study and successfully pass an examination. You must study, as simple as that. This was during the time I was awakened in the middle of the night by a phone call that said, "Bernard has been shot." Devastated by this crisis learning that Bernard had been shot losing his right eye, I ached in my soul as if I had lost a part of my body too. So hurt over this crisis I cried many nights, asking God "why" wanting to let out a scream from the pit of my soul until something happened. This was something I couldn't fix no matter how I wanted to. A mothers' pain is indescribable and when her child suffers, she suffers as well, if not more, emotionally, psychologically, and spiritually.

~Divine Inspiration: Trust God in hard times like never before will draw us nearer to Him.~

The completion of RN school was by the grace of a faithful and loving God giving me strength and faith to hold on and not give up. Trusting and believing in His divine interventions enabled me to see His work in everything. Preparing for state board exam for the second time in my life I attended NCLEX classes, used the hospital library computer and resources, and checked out as many NCLEX books as possible, answering 100 questions everyday for 90 days, three months. I was determined to pass. The exam was computerized and designed to test the graduates' knowledge, skills, and abilities essential for the safe and effective practice of nursing care. After answering 76 questions the computer shut off informing me the exam was complete. It can be a terrifying experience waiting and wondering if you passed the exam. The next two weeks I thought constantly about my results day and night unable to understand why should a student have to wait on results to an exam of such significance. While at work I received a phone call from Monterio saying, "Momma you failed, " then shouted "Just kidding momma you passed." I screamed through the phone so loud the staff at the nurses station all heard my ecstatic joy. I shared the news and Vernita the secretary. She called Terri Marr and within minutes she was on the floor congratulating me with a big hug showing me love. The next day I arrived on the unit she had a banner specially made for me that read "CONGRATULATIONS, CHRISTINE MALONE RN APRIL1999" hanging in front of the nursing station where everybody could see. That was the first time anybody ever shown me special recognition and I will always love and never forget her for that.

~Divine Inspiration: When we include God in everything we do we will have joy and victory. With the power of a made up mind, you are authorized to do anything you choose.~

CHAPTER **26**

Green-Eyed Monster

TRULY ENTHUSIASTIC ABOUT my accomplishments, I thought everybody else would be happy for me too. People from all departments congratulated me, but nurses who worked beside me everyday who knew my struggles and sacrifices never uttered one single word of "congratulations" or "I'm so happy for you" nothing along those lines at all. Nothing! This kind of jealousy is sickening. In the bible it plainly states jealousy is a sin. In Galatians 5:19 the acts of the sinful nature are sexual immorality, impurity and debauchery; idolatry and witchcraft; hatred, discord, jealousy, fits of rage, selfish ambition, dissensions, factions and envy; drunkenness, orgies, and the like. I warn you, as I did before, that those who live like this will not inherit the kingdom of God.

This green-eyed monster, as Shakespeare referred to can camp in our heads at anytime. Therapists often regard the demon as a scar from childhood trauma or a symptom of a psychological problem. It is true that people who feel inadequate, insecure, or overly dependent tend to be more jealous than others. As a young girl I remember many occasions of jealous tendencies from my younger sister. We were so different in our personalities and looked nothing alike. We were like night and day. We got along fairly well as young girls but after adolescence her jealousy for me seem to go to the extreme especially when the opposite sex was involved. She always competed for their attention when it didn't matter one bit to me. Even when dating my ex husband she flirted and flaunted herself in front of him. There was one instance when I was dating a guy and one night we were over to my moms' house and everybody partying, when me and my date started to leave together when she physically attacked me. We fought like cats and to this day I don't know why she attacked me other than the fact, I had a man and she didn't. A man is never worth fighting over and I didn't talk to my sister for weeks.

~Divine Inspiration: Let no gloom dim your vision, but uplift them on high, to the Almighty God in heaven as He smiles on His child in your every storm.~

In a society where being attractive, intelligent, or successful the chances are other women will hate you. What a harsh word but it is what it is. I never really thought I was all of that, but considered myself fairly attractive, thriving everyday to become a better and successful person. Since becoming a career woman my experiences with the green-eyed monster escalated to another level; constantly talked about behind my back, annihilation, catty competition, and looks that kill. I was learning to get joy out of my failures no matter how small. Jealousy is merely an outward reflection of ones deep seated insecurities rooted in poor self image, lack of confidence, fear and insecurity. The only cure for jealousy is to become comfortable with who you are and know God created a magnificent creature in your mother's womb and He loves you just the way you are. I was born to be a unique creature that nobody else can beat me being me. Dealing with the green eyed monster was something I struggled with all my life. I found out late in life you can't win a fight with the devil, so staying clear of people who try to humiliate me in public, ignore nasty and rude comments, and if that doesn't work pull that person over to the side and ask them nicely, "Have I offended you in anyway at all, and if so can I make amends." In essence never having a spirit of jealousy or obsession with this green-eyed monster could not understand why people let this monster take over their lives. The bible says it is a sin and it can literally destroy your soul.

~Divine Inspiration: Divine Inspiration: A tranquil heart gives life to the flesh, but envy makes the bones rot. Proverbs 14:30.~

Terri Marr resigned as nurse manager and started a church with her husband. She will always be remembered as my encourager, supporter, rock, guardian angel who carried me under her wings. God placed her in my life for a season at the right opportune time and I will always be grateful. The new manager Delta a middle aged white woman, short and obese in stature had a stern personality. If you were a RN at Methodist Hospital they allowed you to work the Master Schedule working weekends 7a-7p twelve hour shifts for one month and get paid for forty hours bi-weekly. The next month you worked Monday -Friday 7-3 or 3-11 shift with every weekend off. You alternated this schedule month after month. It was an ideal schedule and no other hospital in the city of-fered it to their RNs.

One particular year Christmas Eve, Christmas Day, New Year Eve, and New Year Day all fell on the weekend the month I was scheduled to work. I approached Delta requesting to change my schedule so I wouldn't work all the holidays but she downright refused stating, "You were the one wanted to work the Master Schedule." I was furious. I missed Terri my guardian angel. She would never make me do something so unfair. I thought how could anyone be so cruel. I even went to talk with her supervisor, but she still didn't change my schedule. I wanted to call in but feared losing my job. I was in the prime of my career and I needed my job. I resented this woman with every ounce of my soul and began looking for a new position in the hospital. Desiring to branch out and find new and better opportunities I applied for a position on 13 Thomas a urology unit. Delta tried sabotaging my transfer but it didn't work.

~Divine Inspiration: If God is for you no weapon forged against you will prevail, and you will refute every tongue that accuses you Isaiah 54:17~

On 13 Thomas I was given one week of orientation then told to charge the whole unit, still a fairly new RN, less than a year, was overwhelming. Meeting significant resistance from other nurses who all seem to hate my existence made it more challenging. For the green-eyed monster to operate in your life you don't have to do any thing, just be successful and God help if you are pretty too. There were two LPNs who deliberately gave me hell every chance they got making things difficult. I prided myself on being able to get along with almost anyone, but when dealing with difficult people it is inevitable confrontations, complaints, criticism will arise quite often.

A charge nurse in a leadership role needs extensive training to handle situations on how to deal with difficult staff that requires more than just tasks and skills but people skills and communication skills too. Most managers choose an experienced nurse with clinical competence and leadership skills to operate a successful unit. Becoming a charge nurse is a difficult role with multi-tasking and the responsibilities it holds is much needed in the hospitals working as frontline managers. An effective charge nurse needs to; incorporate leadership skills which means they commit people to action, convert followers to leaders into change agents, be innovative to take risks, experiment to find new ways of doing things to make the unit a better and safer environment, and role modeling. It has been said by Florence Nightingale that, "Nursing is the finest art."

Charge nurses communicate constantly with doctors, staff, patients, families, supervisors, managers, and other employees. Good communication skills has shown is mostly non-verbal and needs to be done in a tactful, concise, supportive, and none intimidating manner. One of the most difficult skills of most charge nurses is conflict resolution, choosing the passive approach, not addressing the issues directly. Charge nurses first responsibility is the safety of the patients and the accountability to many people solving problems, usually recognizing one before it arises.

Functioning in the charge nurse role was challenging everyday dealing with difficult women who seem to hate who I was and what I stood for; young, black and successful. Becoming a successful black woman created a whole new set of problems in my life. My problem was I wanted to be successful and accepted too, but learned when people not on your level they will try to pull you down every opportunity they get. Being successful caused me to repeatedly encounter haters and repeatedly be attacked. It's a waste of time trying to get along with women who don't like you for no reason at all. If you are not born with thick skin you will get hurt easily. My skin was thin and my feelings were easily hurt working amongst such vindictive and hateful women for almost four months. I decided to apply for a position in the intensive care post operative area.

~Divine Inspiration: Do not fret because of evil doers or be envious of the wicked, for the evil doers has no future hope, and the lamp of the wicked will be snuffed out Proverbs 24:19-20~

The manager Sally Tillsdel personality was incredibly nice and friendly with a pleasant attitude. I felt comfortable approaching her about the position on her unit. Working in the intensive care unit I had an opportunity to get experience and increase my knowledge and clinical skills. I was delighted taking care of acutely and critical ill-patients with a higher acuity levels. The staff was 95% white nurses and snobbishness was detected in the air. With only medical surgical floor nursing experience I was very apprehensive to work in the unit, but was confident and assured that my 13 years of specialized knowledge and skills qualified me. Working in ICU a specialty area nurses respond to life threatening problems in a speedy and compassionate manner is challenging. The nurse ratio was 1:2; or 1:1 depending on the acuity of the patient needing constant monitoring using specialized equipment and medication in order to maintain normal bodily functions.

The only black nurse working on the 7-3 shift was assigned to preceptor Rosalyn Biston RN, who was racist, nasty, distant and aloof, never explaining any procedure or skill thoroughly. A preceptor plays a major role in guiding and supporting nurses transitioning process from one area to another especially for the new graduates during their transition into clinical practice. The preceptor determines if you succeed as a nurse on a particular unit. Working in a high acuity area proper training and a good rapport from a preceptor is important and must be developed to be successful during the orientation process, and I definitely didn't get that from Rosalyn. Once out of orientation with no further support and practically annihilated felt all alone working in a high acuity area that required complex assessment, high intense therapy and interventions from a highly skilled nurse. Instead of support I received sneers, avoidance, write-ups and complaints from nurses. I was called in Sally's office several times to discuss all the write-ups and complaints from the other nurses. She informed me I would need to return to floor nursing. In other words I wasn't competent enough to work in the unit. I am convinced if I had received the proper training and a good rapport from my preceptor Rosalyn things would of turned out differently. But God is my pilot and I shalt not worry.

~Divine Inspiration: Perhaps you were hurt and your heart became hardened as a defense against further pain. God's grace has made provisions for our human weakness, and He is prepared to heal us and teach us to love one another.~

CHAPTER 27

Finding My Place

TRANSFERRING OUT OF ICU to 5A a cardiac unit working with patients suffering from heart diseases and chronic heart conditions. According to the Center of Disease Control, heart disease is the leading cause of deaths in the U.S. of 1.5 million heart attacks occurring each year, and 80 million Americans suffer from heart conditions. Transitioning from a medical surgical nurse to cardiac nurse was challenging and interesting to learn all the different procedures, the different rhythms, and cardiac drugs used to treat patients. For instance 75% of the patients admitted in the hospital experiencing chest pains the first blood test done is cardiac enzymes to get an definitive conclusion of whether it is chest pains or indigestion. Cardiac enzymes are proteins from heart muscle cells released into the bloodstream when the heart muscle is damaged that occurs during a myocardial infarction or heart attack. Some patients are not able to distinguish the difference between a true heart attack and indigestion experience chest pains while taking a deep breathe think they are having a heart attack. The first indication of heart problems are elevated cardiac enzymes which is a significant reason to admit a patient into the hospital. The next test usually done is the exercise stress test performed by a doctor or technician to determine the amount of stress your heart can tolerate before developing either an abnormal rhythm or evidence of ischemia (not enough blood flow to the heart muscle) which usually means blockage in the heart main arteries. This test determine if further evaluation or interventions are needed such as a cardiac catheterization. Cardiac catheterization a procedure where a long thin flexible catheter is inserted into a blood vessel through the groin, arm or neck and thread it to the heart to see if there are significant blockages to the heart muscle. The heart is an amazing organ and I loved to learn about the procedures used to diagnose and treat patients. Usually every procedure possible is used before a coronary artery bypass graft is performed. Most patients do well but it requires longer hospitalization and recovery period.

Currently with an Associate Degree in Nursing on this unit were wonderful nurses full of knowledge, expertise, and compassion. Nursing is a profession that allows nurses to interact with patients physically, emotionally and psychologically. I truly believe, even through all the pain, rejection, failures and struggles I have found my true potential and strength being a nurse and service to others. I enjoy the autonomy and the leadership role as a licensed professional to take care of my patients. Nurses who had their Bachelors Degree in Nursing carried it with such pride. Student nurses did clinical rotations throughout the year on our unit and when asked to be a preceptor by the clinical instructor at the University of Memphis I was thrilled she wanted me to teach and train her students. That planted a seed in me for a desire to teach.

~Divine Inspiration: For every step we take toward our dream God will take two. If we had to do it all on our own, there would be nothing left for God to do for us~

After the seed was planted the desire begin to sprout in me to be an educator which required a Bachelor Degree. I applied at Union University and was accepted. While continuing to work on 5A cardiac unit on the weekend shift and attending nursing school it was a challenge but I loved every bit of it. People asked me why are you going back to school? They even tried to discourage me. I believe when you cease to grow you begin to die. I still desired to reach a higher level of knowledge in my nursing career and refused to listen to the negative things people said. There was so much more I wanted to learn about nursing. I loved being a nurse, a higher and better expression of myself and considered myself to be a life long learner. What else do I have if I don't value me as a person? I am the most valuable thing that I have in life to invest in. During the times when my boys were young, I denied, jeopardized and put my own needs aside to provide for them. Now it was my time to invest in becoming the best person I could possibly become believing nothing is more important than being a whole, loving, healthy human being.

~ Divine Inspiration: If God give you the vision He will give you the provision. Allow faith to replace doubt and let your vision pull you to your victory.~

Nurses all around struggled with "nurse burnt out" and wanted to change their careers. Instead I was advancing my career and didn't understand how could they be burnt out from a career like nursing. Nurse burnt out occurs when the physical and emotional stress of being a nurse get to be too much. The stress can lead to physical and emotional symptoms and lead to professional dissatisfaction. The overall stress can cause a nurse to become dissatisfied with their career if they never concentrate on advancing their career through education to broaden different opportunities. Nursing has many areas of specialties to offer and I wanted to be all I could be in my nursing career, believing with the Sovereignty of God all things are possible.

My faith escalated to a new level by overcoming trials endured in my life; low self esteem, domestic abuse, single parenting, welfare, LPN school, RN school and drug addiction. I learned that faith comes in different levels: *weak faith*, which constantly limits God, *temporary faith* which is when we receive God's word and believe, but fails when test comes *and active faith* is faith without works is dead. "What good is it , my brothers and sisters, if someone claims to have faith but has no deeds? Can such faith save them? (James 2:14), *strong faith* is faith that does not stagger to God's promises, *great faith* has a great expectation, just hearing the word is enough, *perfect divine faith* is absolute confidence in God's own word and being. Our faith gain support and encouragement from whatever has occurred in our past.

~Divine Inspiration: Our faith and God are connected and God will not lead us beyond our present level of trust and obedience to Him~

CHAPTER **28**

Gifted

NOW THAT I was turning forty-five, considered middle-age, I was hoping my best life is before me if I remain steadfast, just endure and not give up, believing God's plan for my life will be worked out in His due time. Older women are Jewels in the crown of Heaven who offer gifts that no one else can. "Charm is deceitful and beauty is passing but a woman who fear the Lord, she shall be praised. A virtuous woman is a woman of honor and integrity and what greater prize I strive to become. A woman who has come from disgrace to grace, determined to keep the light in my heart burning brightly for the career I believe I was called. I was beginning to understand I am a unique expression of life, not a mistake, a right to be who I am, exactly as I am, and no need to prove my worth to others in order to convince myself.

~Divine Inspiration: Once we are prepared and gain the qualities to reach our dream, nothing will keep us from it once His timing is right~

Accepting and acknowledging the presence of God's love

in me and for me there will never again be a doubt in my mind about whether or not I am worthy. For the first time I was beginning to feel good about myself. My flower was blossoming, my self-worth and self-esteem had risen to a new level. Most of my life as a young girl felt overlooked and pushed to the side believing my mother loved my siblings more developed low self-esteem and self worth. I thought my mother treated me different because I looked so much like my father whom she seem to hate. My father always treated me like his little princess and the day we were reunited back with him I was ecstatic.

~Divine Inspiration: There is nothing more validating than believing in your dream, yourself and your abilities~

Instead of listening to all the negative talks and strange looks from people I turned a deaf ear and restrained from sharing my goals. The only people interested in my conversation were the people who were after the same goals as me. It is true birds who flock together have the same interest is who you should surround yourself with. Whenever you are pursuing your dreams you literally have to learn to ignore your naysayers, who will every chance they get try to shoot darts to deflate the air out of your dream. Accomplishing my dream and becoming a nurse in healthcare is exactly where God has led me which has truly been rewarding, fulfilling and made an enormous impact on my life. Nursing has empowered me to care for the sick and disabled and fulfill an obligation to myself, to the medical profession, and to society. God has given me a heart of compassion, mercy, patience, kindness, a good listener, virtues very well needed to provide excellent care to the sick and needy. Determined and willing to persevere to become competent and knowledgeable for which I had been called, I continued to pursue my career in nursing.

God had granted me this gift and to develop it and cultivate this gift is my way to bless him (1Corinthians 7:7).Each man has his own gift from God; one has this gift; another has that(1 Peter 4:10)each one should use whatever gift he has received to serve others, faithfully administering God's grace in its various forms. We can't earn spiritual gifts or deserve them, that is why they are called gifts. They're an expression of God's grace. "Christ has generously divided out his gifts to us." (Ephesians 4:7). Nor do we get to choose which gifts we would like to have. Paul explains that God determines that.

. ~*Divine Inspiration: "It is the one and only Holy Spirit who distributes these gifts. He alone decides which gift each person should have." 1Corinthians 12:11~*

Gifted is when a person's ability is exceptional with a special skill that many do not possess. The discipline of nursing is centered around serving others in a time of need and doing God's will receiving a satisfying and rewarding sense of accomplishment. This just confirms and vindicates why I was led to Christ to become a Christian. You have to be a Christian to want to serve others laying your desires to the side and allowing others to go before you. Pursuing my BSN career while working full-time on 5A, I encountered many struggles and challenges along the way. There was a desire and longing to become more, pushing my way forward diligently with all I had to complete my degree and become an educator. After completing Licensed Practical Nursing and Associate Degree in Nursing I wondered what more could there possibly be left to learn in nursing.

~Divine Inspiration: I will give you every place where you set your feet as I promised Moses. I am keeping you for the moment when you will quickly and confidently bring me glory. Joshua 1:3~

Pursuing a BSN degree in nursing I discovered a whole new level of nursing I never knew existed. The theories and clinical components of nursing and the curriculum consisted of six core competencies: 1). Communication- the need to know how to communicate effectively with the healthcare team, which is very important when trying to convey very important pertinent information. 2) Analytical skills- nursing integrates mathematics, scientific knowledge, and research with nursing practice. 3) Citizenship- nursing demonstrates the ability to meet personal needs as a mature adaptable member within the nursing profession. 4) Critical and creative thinking- nursing demonstrates the ability to think critically and creatively in the identification, analysis, and resolution of problems, issues, truth claims, and ethical issues. 5) Cultural literacy and heritage- nursing understands and appreciates the humanities, social sciences, and fine arts within a global and multicultural society. 6). Concentration- nursing demonstrates the ability and commitment to practice nursing within the roles of provider and manager of care.

These were some of the theoretical and evidence based knowledge discovered during my BSN Degree. Nursing is a phenomena and it has been said it is a professional discipline that is complex, varied, and undermined. Nursing described by Florence Nightingale, founder of the discipline of nursing during the 1860's, as the finest of the Finest Arts. Her measure of nursing incorporated in the care of patients, such as proper noise level, lighting, cleanliness and nutrition. She could not have predicted the evolution of the nurse's role into educator of scientific information, administrator and evaluator of complex treatments, and operator of complex technologies. Today nursing is as much "a science as it is an art." Graduating on May 24, 2004 in Jackson Tennessee on the main campus I realized nursing in part reflects a scientific side of my profession and honestly believed all nurses need a certain degree of scientific knowledge to grasp the understanding of the human body, emotionally and physically regardless of the level of practice he or she might be in her career. Obtaining my BSN Degree has taught me that nursing is an art ultimately found in the everyday management of a sick room with a dying individual or just someone who needs a friendly face to talk to and this is what distinguishes us from all the other professionals of the healthcare team. The nurse has a comprehensive oversight of all the disciplines that converge in the sick room today: medicine, nutrition, social work, pharmacy, physical therapy all who coordinate care providing these essential services.

~Divine Inspiration: We have some gifts inside that would not have been discovered if not for our trials and tribulations. You should be joyful when you encounter various trials because trials produce spiritual endurance and maturity. James:1:2. Each of us has our own unique beauty that God has designed for our lives to create fruitfulness and purpose.~

Upon completion of my Bachelor Degree, my base knowledge expanded and improved my nursing practice to a new level of nursing which included evidence based research. Evidence based research has proven to provide quality patient

GIFTED ❧

care and it takes a multidisciplinary team of professionals to work together to provide compassionate safe quality care. Today nurses are trained in data collection and reporting, work with electronic medical records, drugs, calculators, diagnostic equipment, and new tools of medicine, yet nursing is still a balance between an art and a science. The art of nursing can be thought of as the intentional creative use of oneself based upon skills and expertise, to transmit emotion and meaning to another human being. It also can be thought of as subjective and requires interpretation, sensitivity, imagination, and active participation. Pursuing a Bachelors Degree was worth it, bringing me unexpected benefits in areas of knowledge and professionalism, which led me to become a more effective change agent and patient advocate with the anticipation and goal to become an educator or even taking on a managerial role.

Obtaining a BSN Degree prepared me for a leadership role, raising my self-esteem and confidence, developed and sharpen my critical thinking, exposure to research, holistic nursing, community nursing and changed the way I practiced and viewed nursing. While integrating evidenced based nursing theories and evidence based practice I gained a better awareness of patients' needs emotionally and physically. Having a strong drive and desire to become a better human being a part of my natural make-up was to strive and progress to the next level. We all have that next level to climb whether we choose to or to remain stagnant where we are. Nursing is not one of the highest paid professions but provided a substantial income for me and my two sons. Nursing is not the perfect profession with some flaws such as the hours can be terrible, the staffing is always short, nurses are not appreciated or valued for what we do, and of course we are underpaid.

~Divine Inspiration: Living in a world of corruption you cannot get to where you are going until you have learned all God has for you to learn where you are at this moment.~

All in all I believe if nursing were a majority male occupation nurses would be getting paid higher salaries. In essence, if you love your nursing career you take the good with the bad, the satisfaction and rewards of caring for people making a positive impact versus working long hours without enough staff to cover the unit safely. I love to console and comfort the family members when they are at a point in their lives they do not know what to do or the right questions to ask the doctor. I love the everyday challenge and rewards each day in a fast paced environment using my nursing skills to make someone feel better. But the experience I love dearly and light my hearts' fire is when I am out in public running errands or shopping and one of my patients walk up to me and thank me for the wonderful care I provided while they were a patient in the hospital.

CHAPTER **29**

Open Doors

NURSES WITH EXCELLENT leadership skills are critically important when caring for the sick. Today there are more acute patients due to advanced technology and patients are living longer than they were 10 years ago. After the completion of my BSN Degree a new management position PCC, Patient Care Coordinator, was incorporated in the hospital which is similar to an assistant nurse manager. When I approached my nurse manager to discuss the position she seem to evade the discussion later learning she offered the position to a middle aged white nurse who also held a BSN Degree. Very disappointed that I was not even considered for the position began looking for another position on a different unit. I applied for a PCC at Methodist Germantown Hospital on the 3rd floor, a telemetry/oncology/cardiac/med-surgical specialty unit. A call from the manager Agnes Lester the following week asked me to come in for an interview. During the interview with a well prepared resume, a nice professional cover letter of introduction, dressed in my black pin striped suit with black pumps I felt confident and ready to take on the world. Arriving on time met Miss Lester in the hospital lobby shaking hands after an introduction and then proceeded to the unit for a quick tour of the floor as she introduced me to some of the staff in passing.

~Divine Inspiration: When one door closes in your face, God opens another allowing certain trials in your life to equip you for what He has for your future.~

Immediately following the tour we entered her office and proceeded with the interview with her asking the same questions I had heard many times before during an interview using nurse scenarios situations. What would you do in a nurse patient situation? How would you handle conflicts between co-workers on the unit? Give and example of how to display being a team player. After 16 years of nursing feeling confident I knew there is always more than one answer to any clinical situation. Each nurse is unique and giving your best answer followed with a rationale is the correct answer always. After the interview she asked me when would I like to start. I was totally surprise. I guess she was highly impressed.

~Divine Inspiration: The Land of God's promises is open before us and it is His will for us to possess it, by measuring off the territory with the feet of obedience.~

My first day in my PCC role my supervisor trained me in her office going over my job description and her expectations. She placed extreme emphasis on how to deal with the staff, customer service issues, and making out the schedule for the nurses, and how to counsel and write up disciplinary actions on staff. My job description was assistant manager, along with being charge nurse, and staff nurse occasionally. There were four hired in this position two for day shift, one for night shift and one for weekend shift each of us working three 12 hour shifts. My first day transitioning into this new role there was a strong awry of animosity, encountering resistance and opposition from the nursing staff. This behavior continued and the only time they were cordial or friendly is when they needed me to do something, otherwise the attitudes were horrific. My composure and professionalism were always under a scope and if I said or did anything they thought that could bring me down they ran straight to my manager to report me. In this managerial role I was scrutinized, challenged, insulted, frustrated, and annihilated daily.

~Divine Inspiration: Never fret because of evil doers for like the grass they will wither; like the green plants they will soon die away. Psalm 37:1-2~

The position highly demanding, multidimensional and multitask was one of the most challenging roles in my nursing career. Nurse managers are the most influential force in the healthcare industry and expected to oversee the daily demands of the unit while developing an environment that promotes nursing excellence and foster an engaged staff. This sometimes isn't enough and the position becomes frustrating, overwhelming, and demanding, becoming a position that is harder and harder to fill. Managing people can be extremely stressful and challenging, as a result, causing management to be one of the most complex position in the healthcare industry. Even though we were required to go through a precursor course to prepare us for the role, there is nothing like hands on experience. It is important to have all the tools necessary to become a successful manager to manage difficult people, how to manage the budget, delivering presentations, and sharp communications skills. The exceptional manager knows their own strengths, skills and shortcomings, talents, skills and understand their staff in order to have safe quality care on the unit. This being my first managerial role realized my peoples' skills needed developing to properly manage people.

I was reprimanded several times on how to speak to the staff and be aware of my tone of voice, found it extremely hard not to respond or react to the attacks from the staff making my job difficult. Overall I felt I was doing a great job and Lord knows I tried extremely hard but my haters was around every corner wanting to see me fail. They made my job difficult because I was qualified and they weren't. In a frontline leadership position which carried an immense amount of responsibilities; hiring and firing staff, judging competency of staff, taking overall responsibility for the delivery of safe, high quality patient care, high patient satisfaction, positive patient outcome, managing staff, making assignments, making schedules and even working as a staff nurse when short staffed was frustrating and overwhelming.

~Divine Inspiration: Trials, battles, attacks, and persecution lie in our paths and are to be counted not as misfortunes but rather our necessary training.~

Working diligently trying to prove to my manager I was the right person for the job and that she needed me on her team to operate her unit effectively and not regret the day she hired me. Deliberately putting an effort in having a pleasant attitude with staff when I knew deep down they hated my guts was the second hardest thing I've ever had to do. Never complaining and working consistently throughout the day occasionally coming in early and always leaving late performed quality work with pride. Never sacrificing a patients' safety, and on numerous occasions going above and beyond the call of duty. Being a manager is not easy. Absolutely not! It is a challenge and a major test every single day to deal with difficult people. Difficult people are no problem when passing them on the streets, or standing behind them in line at the supermarket, but when you have to work with them on a regular basis they can be an irritant. As time past I began to feel confident managing the unit and my manager presented me with a card expressing her appreciation for transitioning into my new position and operating a very busy unit satisfactory gave a boost in my confidence.

Managing an oncology/telemetry/medical surgical unit required knowledge, skills, clinical expertise, critical thinking skills, excellent communication skills, professionalism, flexibility and guts. Dealing with difficult people constantly reporting to the supervisor day after day was annoying, tiring and unpleasant. The more she listened to their complaints the more they complained. I thought why isn't she supporting me? Can't she see how difficult this staff is? Can't she see how hard I'm trying? It seemed the more she listened to their lies, half truths, write-ups encouraged my haters even more. I had no friends to confide in and felt the whole unit was against me which is not uncommon in a workplace working with majority women. Former President Harry Truman said, "It is a harsh soil to cultivate the plant of friendship. If you want a friend get a dog." I always thought you had to do something to make enemies but that is farthest from the truth. They all wanted me fired and nothing less would satisfy them more. Working in a leadership position you will cultivate enemies and you can count on them to work against you regardless of your behavior.

~Divine Inspiration: In the pressures of life, guard your heart and know that when God delays, He is not inactive. This is when He prepares you and matures your strength.~

After several counseling sessions with my manager following the write ups she informed me I was not meeting expectations and would have to demoted to a staff nurse position. Heartbroken and humiliated that she was taking away what I had worked so had to hold on to walked away feeling victimized and alienated. My haters had convinced her that I wasn't doing my job when actually I was doing more than enough. I knew I couldn't bear the thought of working as a staff nurse on this unit giving my haters the satisfaction to grin in my face. I contacted a former nurse manager Charlene Rosa at Methodist University and informed her about the situation and asked if I could get my old job back. She said, "Yes." I was very grateful to Mrs. Rosa for understanding when my back was against the wall but fortunately I knew my job history spoke for itself; reliability, professionalism, dependable, conscientious nurse who cared about her patients. No one had to tell me what an excellent nurse I was finding myself everyday fighting on the battle field against the enemy Mrs. Nelms had forewarned me about years ago. A sense of peace and a burden lifted off my shoulders returned to a staff nurse position my first love. A Bachelor Degree of Nursing taught me nursing is just important in a bedside nursing position as it is in a frontline leadership position because nursing is an art or a science.

~Divine Inspiration: The Lord is my strength and my defense~

CHAPTER **30**

The Highest Yet

WORKING AS A staff nurse on 5A Tower striving to be all God created me to be enrolled in the University of Phoenix online program. The more I learn the more I want to learn believing the day you stop learning you become stale and stagnant, lose creativity, initiative, and your professional spark. Learning is a lifelong process and never ceases in any career. It is impossible to learn all there is to know in any profession in a two to four year degree program. You are always learning something new everyday and continuing education is required in all healthcare institutions to keep abreast of all the new research and changes occurring all the time. Desiring to further my education to enhance my emotional, physical, and spiritual aspects of patient care also stemmed back to that dreadful day in LPN school when an instructor told me I wasn't nursing material and should consider choosing another profession but instead chose to trust and believe in God. What she meant for evil God allowed to instill a fire for nursing and education that never goes out.

I eagerly enrolled in University of Phoenix online program in 2005 looking forward to adding new knowledge to my knowledge base. I understood knowledge is worth more than gold. Knowledge is power. Knowledge can carry you a long way in this world. The recruiters were awesome providing their support guiding me through the enrollment process so graciously that it was very difficult to change my mind. I was given the option to fit my school schedule around my work schedule and personal life making everything so convenient and easy for me providing their services 24/7 seven days a week to help me on my new nursing journey. They even made courtesy calls occasionally to see how I were adjusting. All the recruiters were committed to a mission that asked four questions: 1) Do you know what you should know? 2) Can you do what you should be able to do? 3) Have we helped you develop values that are appropriate to my profession. 4) Are you achieving your life and career goals? With the support and guidance of UOP made it so easy to pursue my MSN Degree online.

~Divine Inspiration: God creates power in our lives by creating pressure. He uses the pressure to generate power to rise above the painful circumstances that produced it.~

The UOP online program offered courses in a format you can take anytime or anywhere which mirrored a classroom. The courses are taught by part-time faculty practitioners who post lectures every week and class participants use synchronous threaded discussions and email as primary communication mode to complete assignment and give feedback. Education became my area of interest after experiencing the managerial role thinking education might be a better fit for me. Going through an online program was the most incredible way to receive an education and I will never choose the traditional classroom setting again. My educational process developed a change in my vocabulary and conceptual thinking skills, enhancing my BSN knowledge base and skills, addressed functioning in a leadership role in practice and educational settings learning how to perform detailed assessments and evaluations, write objectives, create educational programs, and learn educational strategies.

~Divine Inspirations: My grace is sufficient for you. Little faith will bring your souls to heaven, but great faith will bring heaven to your souls.~

Charlene Rosa was an easygoing manager, never giving me any problems or hassle about the little stuff. Then one day she was let go because she refused to go back to school to receive her BSN degree which was required to hold a managers' position. She left Methodist to work for Home Health Nursing leaving our unit without a manager quickly replaced by an interim Della Tolliver from 9A Tower. The word was going around she was hired to get rid of all the troublemakers. When she spoke it was like a knife cutting right through your heart, intimidating, demeaning, with such a cold demeanor. She appeared to enjoy coming off as an intimidating bully with a berating disposition. In her office sitting across from her at her desk her bulging eyes seemed to penetrate my soul. Without an ounce of compassion or empathy, whenever there was allegations brought against me I was never given an opportunity to dispute the allegations. The third time in her office I sensed something wasn't right that entire day. I sat across from her desk she read off allegations that were not true and someone even forged my initials on one of the forms she set before me to sign. The more I tried to dispute the allegations the bigger those bulging eyes got. Then she threatened me to quit before I get fired suggesting I try working in a slower pace environment. She was a snake in the grass with a heart of ice.

~Divine Inspiration: Afflictions are often the dark settings God uses to ascend His children and their gifts, causing us to shine even brighter opening our hearts in the shadows of life.~

In just three short months this woman had come in and literally forced me to quit my job of 20 years. Slowly emptying my locker and leaving the facility walking to my car totally numb asked God, " How could this be happening? Am I suppose to fight for my job?" I did not have any more fight in me. I had fought for 20 years and I was tired. Tired of defending. Tired of justifying. Tired of the lies. All I wanted to do was go home and surrender it all to God. I learned you can't fight the Devil. I wondered how could she have the gall to ask me to leave my job when I hadn't caused a death or jeopardized the life and safety of a patient. But the Devil never has a legitimate reason to come after God's Chosen, they just do. Some nurses in authority walk around with the face of stone hiding behind a mask due to insecurity. I wondered if my pursuit of my Master Degree intimidated her in anyway. After a week of my departure from Methodist the stress in my life subsided and I rested in the Lord realizing nothing happens unless he allows it for whatever His reasons may be. The year 2009 was a turning point for my life in a new direction. God had allowed everything that happened in my life to prepare me to go down a different path. My testimony in church was how God has provided and never forsaken me even when the enemy thought they had the victory. Truly I was the one with the victory with God opening doors to bigger and better things in my future. I continued to work PRN status for Baptist Hospital and researched on how to start my own business. Focusing on completing my MSN degree I refused to stay down no matter how many times the Devil tried to block my blessings.

~Divine Inspiration: Keep looking up. With all the distress, depression, discouragement, all around your feet, Jesus Our Lord, will defeat when looking up~

~Divine Inspiration: One who trust and believe in God's promises knows that all the riches abiding in them as his own.~

Now that I was no longer working for Methodist I focused on completing my MSN Degree which required long hours of research and reading to write graduate level papers. Graduate level papers requires a strong thesis statement, body paragraphs to support the thesis, and evidence of having researched the topic. The papers had to be as long as 5000-7800 words and must be free of grammatical errors, concise and clear in order for it to be a quality graduate level work. All the online instructors had a Master Degree in Education with previous teaching online experience. When the course began they would introduce themselves by posting a photo and an extensive biography expounding on their educational demographic and work background sharing about their families and hobbies. The students were required to do the same but posting our photo was an option. Reading all the biographies of the instructors and the other students was an interesting way to meet people and made it a more personal environment.

CHAPTER **31**

Business Minded & Instructor

OBTAINING MY MSN Degree came with many challenges, sacrifices, and detours but when I look back I will never regret the journey that offers so many career opportunities. A Master Degree gave me a different perspective in the world of nursing, an opportunity to be in an environment with other professionals learning to build critical interpersonal skills and broadening our knowledge. Ultimately I was gaining a sense of satisfaction that facilitated personal and professional growth while becoming a better nurse, a better person I never could of imagine. Desiring to start my own business was a part of that growth and I looked into how to start a home care agency providing care for seniors and disabled individuals in the privacy of their homes. Due to the aging population and many Americans preferring to be cared for in their homes, starting my own agency to meet this great demand for home care can be a rewarding opportunity. A non-medical home care service includes personal care, assistance with daily living activities, meal preparation, housekeeping, and transportation. Being a nurse really wasn't a prerequisite, but strong communication and organizational skills with a well planned business strategy is what a business needs to be successful. Jumping into a business without a plan is asking for failure. Without any experience in the business arena I thought getting a office was more important than having a successful business plan. With love and passion for nursing strongly believed after receiving an advanced educational background there was a great need for home care in the community. With no business plan put forward and poor management skills, lacking expertise in areas such as finance, purchasing, selling, production, and hiring and managing employees starting a business was very challenging.

Even after leaving my 20 nursing career God provided me the grace, strength and determination to continue my advanced educational degree. After graduating I looked for an educational position that interest me. Teaching is a integral part of nursing and becoming a nurse educator was a natural step for me with many years of nursing experience. Although there is a significant shortage of nurse educators, this also impacts the number of student nurses to become prepared nurses in the healthcare industry. Whether in the classroom or the clinical setting I wanted to contribute and give back to nursing students and the opportunity to work alongside educators dedicated to advancing the nursing profession through advance education. I knew teaching nursing students would instill in me a joy and satisfaction of returning a treasured gift of knowledge and skills to future nurses. While searching for a part-time job I continued researching about operating my own business successfully. UOP taught me the importance of strong communication and organization skills with a well planned business strategy to succeed in operating my own business. They taught me how to write a business plan including an executive summary, market analysis including industry outlook, a list of employees and their skills and qualifications, and a financial summary. This instilled a seed to never give up on my dream to own my own business in home health care or home care and the importance of a well written plan in order to be successful.

~Divine Inspiration: Return to God and trust Him to meet the needs in your life that only He can. Allow Him to complete His work in you and see what fruit your life produces.~

Updating my resume was well overdue and began my search for a part-time educator position. I no longer desired to work fulltime with a long term goal to establish my own business. Applying for a part-time instructor position at Tennessee Technical Vocational Center I was hired by Mrs Theresa Yarbrough, the coordinator of the program to teach LPN students. Mrs. Yarbrough also had a Master Degree in Education and many years of nursing experience. Being an instructor teaching practical nursing students, there were many challenges sometimes I felt like a mother hen to adult kids in a classroom with their only goal being to get through this program. Staring into the faces of women of all ages who desperately wanted to become nurses, hungry for a chance to make a better life for themselves I saw myself. With them there weren't any room for racism because all the instructors were black making it better for them. There was no white middle age instructor building walls for young black women making the program extremely difficult because she can't stand the fact black women want an education too. Black women do not want to depend on welfare their whole lives and deserved the right to be treated equally if they put forth an effort to want a better life for themselves. The class consisted of 55 students; 53 blacks and 2 whites, the majority on welfare allotted grants providing an educational opportunity.

After the end of WWII the government saw a dire need for more nurses in the healthcare industry so they instigated the Licensed Practical Nurse (LPN) program. LPNs has a noble history starting in the 1940s as a way to get licensed caregivers into the workforce in a shorter period of time, compared to registered nurses. For the past several decades there has been efforts to eliminate the LPN role in the healthcare system. There were even times when the LPNs and nursing assistants were released from all hospitals and the RNs were responsible for total care. Today most hospital are leaning toward hiring only RN and LPNs are encouraged to return back to school to complete their nursing degree in a RN program with excellent reimbursement benefits. The supply and demand data for LPNs varies, depending on the location, area of practice, scope of practice, and whether unlicensed personnel can be utilized in the place at a cheaper cost to the employer.

> ~Divine Inspiration: Your goal is the what of your life, the purpose is the why of your life, and your mission is the how of your life, then once these are clear, you have a focus for your life.~

In the classroom setting students try to manipulate their way to get a passing grade every opportunity they can trying to convince me their answer is the best answer even when the answer key say otherwise. When an answer was checked incorrect on their exam the rationale for the correct answer did not matter to them, they only wanted their answer to be right, always trying to hustle a point. There were rules in grading exams. If over half the class missed the same questions the whole class would receive credit for that particular question. I totally agreed with this policy. It was stressful and paralyzing handling situations when the whole class came at you at the same time. My Director was always there giving me guidance, support and advice on how to deal with conflict in the classroom. Working only two days a week and when the semester ended my Director approached me about taking on a full-time position teaching but I declined and continued working PRN status at Baptist with the dream of operating my own business. Teaching is a very demanding job that requires many hours of reading and preparation to give effective lectures in the classroom. Being able to manage a classroom of unruly students is very stressful.

~Divine Inspiration: We have the power to choose, to create what we want in our lives. All we have to do is see it, it must come to past. That is God's Universal Law.~

Not really finding what I wanted at Tennessee Vo-Tech Center applied at Baptist School of Nursing teaching BSN students into a part-time adjunct clinical instructor position. The education of BSN students require a balance between theoretical knowledge and clinical preparation and considered the science and art of nursing. I received a brief three day orientation to being the instructor of eight BSN students. Going from teaching LPN students to BSN students is a higher and advanced level of teaching requiring various tasks; organization, even-tempered, multi-tasking. Despite having over twenty years of nursing experience I realized I only had half the knowledge and expertise required to manage and discipline BSN nursing students. Learning how to relate to a group of students where there is a generational gap, developing a relationship with the staff as an educator instead of as a staff nurse, making clinical assignments, planning and facilitating pre- and post conferences, clinical evaluations, and being accountable ensuring each student provide safe and effective nursing care was overwhelming.

Engaging in a teacher-student interpersonal relationship required patience, tact, insight and endurance to become a successful educator. I learned early in my career I lack a very important element in my social and people skills, the like-ability factor, which has led to hardship and struggle in my career. Advance education broaden my opportunities for higher level positions requiring me to enhance my interpersonal and social communication skills. After teaching a class for eight hours was like I had an intense physical and emotional workout, stretched, pulled and emotionally challenged at every angle. Learning to shift my actions as a nurse from the delivery of quality care of patients to the delivery of quality education to students as an educator was a learning experience for me.

~Divine Inspiration: God allow strong and constant pressures to show us His all sufficient strength and grace and bring us to a greater awareness of our dependence on Him.~

Social skills create powerful hidden factors that often can create your chances for promotion in your career without your awareness you are capable of achieving. When human professionals are asked what keeps talented people from moving up, they often cite personality, the perception of inflexibility, poor people skills and often overlooked the lack of the like-ability factor. Some people tend to sideline their careers by being focused on skills that require a good deal of expertise but the lack of the like-ability factor is very prevalent in the workplace and society and play a major factor in promotions and other successes on the job. I found myself being skilled and competent but disliked by most of your co-workers falling short of this like-ability factor, that happens quite often while working amongst majority women occupations.

My performance as a nurse was excellent; emotionally caring, understanding, compassionate, non-judgmental, and strong ability to empathize with patients from all cultures and nationalities. Patients look to me not only to treat their illness but to educate and offer support to them and family members as well; intellectually I am intelligent, organized, good at multitasking, recording patient history asking the right questions to get the correct information; effective communications skills with doctors, patients, and co-workers in a fast paced environment, reporting off to nurses on patients' conditions, keen observational skills, any change in patient's behavior, any cuts or wounds, excellent clinical skills; inserting IV's, transfusions, charting correctly, moving and transferring patients when needed. With all these wonderful attributes and skills why is the like-ability factor missing? The like-ability factor is a powerful tool. Most of the time when women manifest success, intelligence in a leadership role they are punished and disliked but men are rewarded. Interpersonal social skills are the competencies used for interaction and effective communication with other people, can make or break one's career. We learn these skills in our families and among our peers. Someone who has solid interpersonal social skills listens actively, speak clearly, communicate with efficiency, regulate one's emotions, build rapport, and resolve conflicts. Possessing all these attributes but without the like-ability factor faced a series of uphill battles in my personal and professional life.

Divine Inspiration: Accept and acknowledge your own brilliance. Stop waiting on other people confirmation. Stop waiting on others to tell you how great you are. Seek to bring every desire under the control of the spirit accomplishing what God promised. Believe in yourself.~

A nurse educator is an important part of the medical team preparing nursing students for the role in the nursing profession. The more clinical experience the nurse educator has increases the effectiveness of her teaching skills to student nurses. Clinical practice in nursing programs provides the means for students to develop knowledge, cognitive and technological skills and a value system to care for patients. Students learn effective methods of reasoning and approaching patient problems and become socialized in the profession. In this role as an clinical educator, proud to share my knowledge and expertise to students in the clinical setting preparing them for present and future practice in the nursing profession. This job offered me a harmonious blend of nurturing and education, the best of both worlds, the unique and wonderful opportunity to teach students in an extremely challenging, stressful and demanding profession. Being a novice the weight of the unreasonable demands from the administration, increasing clinical site requirements, shared governance duties, papers and care plans to grade was overwhelming. Learning to balance everything would take some time to find a rhythm and develop multifaceted skills necessary to confidently to fill this role. Determined to be the best teacher I could possibly be students reported me saying I was too strict and unfair. My supervisor informed me certain situations were handled in an inappropriate manner with no understanding, empathy, support, or effective mentoring, while the overwhelming demands continued. After that semester I did not return for the following semester. To become a clinical instructor time and experience is imperative for a staff nurse transitioning into this new role to learn the duties and values of the role. Despite the challenges, the rewards of teaching are many, immensely satisfying to witness fledging students mature into competent nursing graduates.

~Divine Inspiration: Sail away! Spread your wings toward the storm trusting in the one who rules over the raging seas. "Put your hope in God." Psalm 42:6~

CHAPTER 32

Nurse Entrepreneurship

I CONTINUED TO work at Baptist while establishing my home care nursing service business. It was time for me to be my own boss, to have creative freedom, to be able to make my own hours, use my knowledge and skills as a platform to advance to the next level of nursing. I know when one door closes God opens another. All those doors that closed in the past was God planting a vision in my heart for something better.

~Divine Inspiration: The moment we get born again God gives us a gift inside of us to carry out His purpose. The one essential quality of the kind of faith to create great things from God is boldness and daring.~

Entrepreneurship is the pursuit of an opportunity and this was my opportunity to excel in nursing with God's help. All of my failures, trials, tribulations where I was rejected, ostracized, humiliated, fired, made to feel inadequate and incompetent only happened because God allowed it and used those roadblocks as stepping stones to prepare me for bigger and better things. In the midst of those trials during some of the worst years of my life I found strength in God to persevere, to make me and not break me. Giving up was never an option. I loved nursing too much. I realized there is a positive aspect to suffering. God was molding me through my suffering perfecting me to come up like shining gold. Even Jesus Christ was complete only after he had endured suffering.

Starting a business choosing the name *Caring Nurses* exemplified who we are and how we do it. Caring is the essence of nursing. A feeling exhibiting concern and empathy for others. Caring is the heart of nursing. Caring is universal and it influences the way people think, feel and act. Benner (Holistic Theory) : equates excellent nursing practice ; caring means connectedness; caring helps people understand and adjust to illness. Nursing is an art, and every nurse to prepare for this takes an exclusive devotion to learn, practice and become experts at the science (technology, interventions, pharmaceuticals) and artistry (therapeutic presence, compassionate care) of our practice. The ultimate aim of caring is to preserve a person's dignity, his/her absolute value as a human being, and the right of self-determination.

~Divine Inspiration: Attempting great things through faith and taking the strength of God to accomplish them, understanding Jesus deepest pain came but he held on to His father's plan for his life.~

Nurses experience a sense of impotence when they are unable to provide care that preserves the patient's dignity which leads to burn out and dropout from the profession. I especially wanted my customers to know that we care about them. After much research I found there are hundreds of other businesses doing what I desired to do. Taking a leap of faith from traditional nursing to a career as a nurse entrepreneurship is a big step which is what faith is, taking that next step knowing that God has your back and that you can not do anything without Him. Once venturing away from bedside nursing thinking I wanted to be an educator but my passion seem to linger toward taking care of the elderly population. This group of people are so vulnerable and most are alone and need help in their everyday living.

My relationship with God had grown to another level and I believed Jesus Christ died for my sins and resurrected from the grave so I could have eternal life. First becoming a Christian in my family church where my mother was a member and my cousin the pastor in 1994. I backslid from the church and rejoined rededicating my life in 2005. A small church with only 30-40 members the Pastor appointed me the secretary and Sunday school teacher that seem to be an ideal life. After being disappointed so many times in the church, rejected by most of the sisters and even the first lady walking the Christian life wasn't easy and not a happy life and wondered why should I enter into something so uncomfortable with so many obstacles to deter me off the path. I became engaged to a brother a relationship that was built on lies and deceit. But with God the truth was revealed.

~Divine Inspiration: It is God's desire to love me, guide me, protect me, provide for me, and shower me with love filled goodness. God desires for me to be happy, healthy and loved.~

In 2012 joining Bellevue Baptist Church intimidated by the size of the church and congregation but with time I easily adapted to the environment. The people were kind and invit-ing. I became involved and joined a Life Group which is the same as Sunday School with a group of women in my age range sharing our life's trials, struggles and praises. Excited to be a part of a church I wanted to serve so I became ac-tive in serving on the Welcome Center greeting people at the entrance answering questions and assisting them in the right direction. I also volunteered as a nurse on some Saturdays at their satellite church Impact taking blood pressures, educat-ing about medication, living a healthy wholesome life, and ministering to people who came to receive free food offered through the church. Even though the church is a ninety per-cent white congregation I realize race will always be an issue in this country but worshipping God with other believers on the same accord is satisfying and fulfilling. I am more accept-ed here for who I am. There were no turning of heads to keep from speaking nor cold stoic looks from my sisters refusing to acknowledge my presence. At Bellevue to be around people who are kind was unbelievable and I have never been happier in a church like Bellevue getting to meet so many people all walks of life.

~Divine Inspiration: There is no way to learn faith except through trials, God's school of faith. Once we learn this, it is everlasting possession and eternal riches.~

CHAPTER **33**

Living a Happy Christian Life

~Divine Inspiration: "For you created my innermost being; you knit me together in my mother's womb. 139:12~

ALL THE DIFFICULT places I traveled through God was giving me the opportunity to exercise and build my faith in Him to bring about blessed results and glory to His name. During the anger, confusion, self doubt, self judgement I wanted to give up but God kept reminding me I was the light and I must shine. This was my job and without the darkness I would have no meaning. Becoming a Christian I was a new creature where old things have passed away and the fullness of Christ began to live in me and I did things differently. No doubt the Christian walk hasn't been easy but I wouldn't trade it for anything else, remembering the shouts of joy when my soul became acquainted with the Lord Jesus and His mighty powers. Becoming a believer everything seem so easy. I was more than a conqueror, through Him that loved me. Finding Jesus as my Savior from the penalty of my sins, reading the scriptures finding much precious truth, and feeding and nourishing my soul, in spite of it all, I searched for that bread and water of life promised in the scriptures that the early Christians Moses, Abraham, Mary, or Ruth enjoyed, possessed, and lived in.

As I continued to walk this Christian walk things seem to grow dim and the best I can expect is a life of alternating failure and victory having to constantly repent all over again. I was beginning to wonder, "Is this all it is to a Christian walk?" Did Jesus lay down His precious life with only this in mind? Did He intend for me to struggle under defeat and discouragement? Did He want my enemies to have dominion over me? Did He mean for me to triumph sometimes and not all the time?

~Divine Inspiration: The Christian life must be looked upon not as an attainment, but as an obtainment. A gift from God.~

The bible tells us that Jesus was manifested that he might destroy the works of the devil and save us from the power and the dominion of sin and we are made conquerors. The Christian life is being hid in Christ, surrendering ourselves doing it gladly, thankfully and enthusiastically finding this the happiest place to be. After surrender the next thing comes faith. Longing to please God and tired of the sin filled life which grieves Him I wanted to be delivered from its powers. Everything I tried had failed; men, drugs, alcohol, promiscuity, lies to satisfy my flesh which led to destruction and now wondered if Jesus was able to deliver me.

To be delivered I had to go through the transformation and the renewing of my mind, sins had to be conquered; evil habits overcome; wrong dispositions and feelings rooted out.

A positive transformation had to take place and I was unable to do it for myself, but the Lord Jesus came and would do it for me if I put myself into His hands and trust Him without restraints. All I needed to do was trust while He did the work. There are many trials and suffering to endure in a Christian walk. I have learned to look at them as God's winds blowing strong against me, His tests taking my life to higher levels and closer to Him. Although being a Christian calls for a significant standards of ministry and high integrity I struggled occasionally with many weaknesses but studied God's word to strengthen my spiritual character to encourage myself when facing severe trials.

~Divine Inspiration: Tribulations produces perseverance, perseverance produces character and character produces HOPE.~

Conquering my sinful nature was a everyday battle growing as a Christian woman preventing me from reaching full spiritual maturity. I come to realize that sin is a persistent, determined and pernicious enemy that robs us of every good thing God wants to give us to have an abundant life. Sin is subtle, it creeps in appearing so attractive that makes us think it can't harm us. I had to come to understand that living in sin is bondage and I will never be able to run the race God has destined for my life as long as I was entrapped by it. I can't blame anyone else for my sins and not allow pride to convince me it is too humiliating to admit the sin in my life. I had to recognize sin for what it was and that it creeps into my life when and where I least expect it.

Yet I found God during my darkest days of affliction and pain which has produced some of the brightest memories of God's enduring presence, His everlasting grace, and love in spite of my solitude and sadness. Becoming a believer in Christ Jesus, a saintly calling, comes the redemption and forgiveness of my sins, along with the responsibility of living a holy life, through the power of the Holy Spirit that dwells inside of me. As I yield to God through prayer and reading of His word daily the characteristics of a true godly woman is being evident in my life, making my life a testimony to living a Christian life. Most people find it almost impossible to live a happy Christian life mainly because they have yet to be delivered from people of the world. They live their lives trying to please people, going over and beyond avoiding to offend or hurt anyone's feeling, or just worrying about what people think about them. This is a severe bondage and if not broken people will never live a life of freedom.

"The joy of the Lord is my strength." Nehemiah 8:10, is my favorite scripture I find strength and joy speaking during distress,despair, and struggles. During some of my darkest moments the Lord has loved me in His measureless devotion, faithfulness and generosity. To be loved by a God like this is hard not to give up everything that is separate from Him, consenting to give up liberty of choice and glory in His nearness which makes me enthusiastically devoted not only possible but necessary. God has made the first and chief commandment that we should love Him with all our might and with all our strength and to come into so close a union to make a separation from the world receiving an unspeakable joy. He makes this offer to everyone, but all do not say yes. Christian life is an unspeakable privilege I have entered with my Heavenly Father following Him wherever He might lead on this spiritual romance making everyday and every hour grand.

CPSIA information can be obtained at www.ICGtesting.com
Printed in the USA
LVOW10s1656050816

498720LV00004B/4/P